Armies of the Crusaders, 1096–1291

Armies of the Crusaders, 1096–1291

History, Organization, Weapons and Equipment

Gabriele Esposito

Pen & Sword
MILITARY

First published in Great Britain in 2023 by
Pen & Sword Military
An imprint of
Pen & Sword Books Limited
Yorkshire – Philadelphia

Copyright © Gabriele Esposito 2023

ISBN 978 1 39906 744 7

The right of Gabriele Esposito to be identified as
Author of this Work has been asserted by him in accordance
with the Copyright, Designs and Patents Act 1988.

A CIP catalogue record for this book is
available from the British Library

All rights reserved. No part of this book may be reproduced or
transmitted in any form or by any means, electronic or mechanical
including photocopying, recording or by any information storage and
retrieval system, without permission from the Publisher in writing.

Typeset by Mac Style
Printed and bound in India by Parksons Graphics Pvt. Ltd.

Pen & Sword Books Limited incorporates the imprints of After the Battle, Atlas, Archaeology, Aviation, Discovery, Family History, Fiction, History, Maritime, Military, Military Classics, Politics, Select, Transport, True Crime, Air World, Frontline Publishing, Leo Cooper, Remember When, Seaforth Publishing, The Praetorian Press, Wharncliffe Local History, Wharncliffe Transport, Wharncliffe True Crime and White Owl.

For a complete list of Pen & Sword titles please contact

PEN & SWORD BOOKS LIMITED
47 Church Street, Barnsley, South Yorkshire, S70 2AS, England
E-mail: enquiries@pen-and-sword.co.uk
Website: www.pen-and-sword.co.uk
or
PEN AND SWORD BOOKS
1950 Lawrence Rd, Havertown, PA 19083, USA
E-mail: uspen-and-sword@casematepublishers.com
Website: www.penandswordbooks.com

Contents

Acknowledgements — vii
Introduction — viii

Chapter 1   The Mediterranean World of the Eleventh Century   1

Chapter 2   The First Crusade   14

Chapter 3   The Second Crusade   51

Chapter 4   The Third Crusade   77

Chapter 5   The Fourth and Fifth Crusades   95

Chapter 6   The Sixth, Seventh and Eighth Crusades   109

Chapter 7   Crusader Armies   121

Bibliography — 157
The Re-enactors who Contributed to this Book — 158
Index — 160

Gabriele Esposito is a military historian who works as a freelance author and researcher for some of the most important publishing houses in the military history sector. In particular, he is an expert specializing in uniformology: his interests and expertise range from the ancient civilizations to modern post-colonial conflicts. During recent years he has conducted and published several researches on the military history of the Latin American countries, with special attention on the War of the Triple Alliance and the War of the Pacific. He is among the leading experts on the military history of the Italian Wars of Unification and the Spanish Carlist Wars. His books and essays are published on a regular basis by Pen & Sword Books, Osprey Publishing, Winged Hussar Publishing and Libreria Editrice Goriziana, and he is also the author of numerous military history articles appearing in specialized magazines such as *Ancient Warfare Magazine*, *Medieval Warfare Magazine*, *The Armourer*, *History of War*, *Guerres et Histoire*, *Focus Storia* and *Focus Storia Wars*.

Acknowledgements

This book is dedicated to my magnificent parents, Maria Rosaria and Benedetto, for the immense love and fundamental support that they always give me. It is thanks to their precious advice, over many years, that this book is even better than I had hoped. A very special thanks goes to Philip Sidnell, the commissioning editor of my books for Pen & Sword: his love for history and his passion for publishing are the key factors behind the success of our publications. Many thanks also to the production manager of this title, Matt Jones, for his excellent work and great enthusiasm. A special mention is due to Tony Walton, for the magnificent work of editing that he makes for all my books. A very special mention goes to the brilliant re-enactment groups that collaborated with their photos to the creation of this book: without the incredible work of research of their members, the final result of this publication would have not been the same. As a result, I want to express my deep gratitude to the following living history associations: Les Seigneurs d'Orient from France, and Ordenskomturei Heppenheim and Sericum et ferrum from Germany.

Introduction

The Crusades were without doubt some of the most important military campaigns that took place during the Middle Ages, witnessing the confrontation between the Christians of Europe and the Muslims of the Middle East in a 'clash of civilizations' that had never before been seen in the Mediterranean. They took place in a period of fundamental historical importance for Western Europe, during which feudalism was dominant and international commerce started to regain most of the importance that it had lost following the fall of the Roman Empire. In this book we will try to describe the military events of the period from 1096–1291, starting with the First Crusade and ending with the fall of the last Crusader strongholds in 1291, paying special attention to analysis of the various political entities that took part in these military and religious expeditions. We will see how the Papacy 'invented' the idea of the crusade and how it organized the various expeditions; at the same time, we will try to understand who the Crusaders were and why these men chose to risk their lives by fighting in the Middle East. As will emerge from the text, the Crusades were not only conducted by aristocratic knights, but saw the participation of many commoners who were moved by their religious zeal. The book will explain why the First Crusade was so successful and how, after it, several Crusader states were established by the Christians in the Levant. These states – the Kingdom of Jerusalem, Principality of Antioch, County of Edessa, County of Tripoli and Kingdom of Cyprus – all had their own peculiar history. The analysis will follow the evolution of the Crusades, showing how such expeditions were initially organized by the major European monarchs before coming under the direct control of the powerful 'Maritime Republics' of Italy. After the Third Crusade, in fact, the original spirit of the armed pilgrimages was progressively lost. We will follow the development of the eight major Crusades, but also the lesser-known ones, for example those organized by commoners – the so-called People's Crusades – which failed so spectacularly. The seventh and final chapter of the book will be dedicated to analysis of the organization and equipment of the Crusader armies, which were extremely complex. The Crusader troops consisted of multi-ethnic contingents: their core was formed by the forces recruited according to the feudal military system, but there were also the famous Military Orders of warrior-monks (which will be covered in full detail) and the native contingents recruited on a local basis by the Crusaders, which could consist of local soldiers in Christian service or of auxiliaries provided by the few regional allies of the Crusader states in the Middle East. The native contingents of the Crusader armies are little-known, but played a significant part in the military campaigns of 1096–1291. Their members, known as Turcopoles, fought with the same tactics and equipment as their Muslim opponents. Similarly little-known are the allied contingents of the Crusader armies, which came from the Christian realms of Armenia and Georgia or were recruited from the Christian minorities of the Holy Land (such as the warlike Maronites of Lebanon). Thanks to the efforts of their military forces, which always experienced great organizational problems during this period, the Crusader states of the Levant were able to survive for a long time, repulsing dozens of Muslim invasions. The book is illustrated with colour reconstructions of the most important troop types that made up the Crusader armies, from the European feudal contingents to the knights of the Military Orders, and from the locally recruited Turcopoles to the peasant infantrymen.

Chapter 1

The Mediterranean World of the Eleventh Century

Around the end of the eleventh century, Western Europe was experiencing the most flourishing period of feudalism and its various states had growing economies. After centuries of partial social and cultural decline, it had entered a new historical phase that was characterized by the prominence of the feudal order and of the Church. At the time of the start of the Crusades, Western Europe was fragmented into a series of semi-autonomous political entities of different dimensions known as fiefdoms. Each of these was dominated by an aristocrat, who was a landowner but also a warrior, fighting as a heavily equipped knight or *miles*, since cavalry dominated the military scene. In the feudal world, war was one of the aristocrats' main occupations and the decisive factor that determined their personal power. No standing armies existed, and thus the nobles were the only components of feudal society who could raise military forces. Society was divided – quite strictly – into three main categories. The first was that of the aristocracy, owning large land properties and having the 'privilege' of exercising violence by the use of arms. The second category was the clergy, who enjoyed a marked moral superiority over the others since they administered the religious rites. The final group were the commoners, who were – for the most part – peasants living and working on the land properties of the nobles. The leading social group – whose members were known as *bellatores* – had effective political power; the second – known as *oratores* – were rich enough and well organized to exert a strong moral influence; the third – the *laboratores* – had very few freedoms and rights. This macro-organization of society could be seen in each local community on a micro level. Within each fiefdom, the political power of the noble landowner was represented by his castle, with the moral power of the clergy evident in the various ecclesiastical buildings. The aristocrats were autonomous in the ruling of their land properties: they collected taxes, obliged their peasants to fight in case of war, controlled commerce and administered justice. Although central governments existed in Western Europe in the form of feudal monarchies, these were extremely weak in comparison with the states of later periods. England and France, together with the Spanish realms of Castile and Aragon, were the most important feudal monarchies in Europe. They were ruled by powerful royal houses – the Plantagenets and the Capetians, respectively – and already ruled extensive territories. The kingdoms of both England and France, however, consisted of many fiefdoms that were ruled by ambitious and powerful nobles, who were more interested in pursuing their own interests than in supporting the central government. Having a weak monarchy corresponded to a higher degree of autonomy on a local scale. Rebellions by feudal overlords against their kings were quite common; the monarchs did not have central armies, having to rely on only small households to protect them. The stability of a realm depended on its monarch's capability to govern with the support of the great nobles, which could only be achieved by renouncing any strong centralized control over the various fiefdoms. The latter, according to the feudal system, varied in size and economic capabilities. Feudalism worked thanks to what was known as the sub-infeudation system, whereby each major fiefdom ruled by an important aristocrat such as a count or duke was sub-divided into a series of minor fiefdoms. The latter could be quite small, consisting of just a castle – controlled by a knight – and its surrounding countryside. The major fiefdoms could cover large territories, comparable to that of a regional state, and could thus field large military contingents, since all their minor fiefdoms were required to provide men for the formation of their overlord's army. On most occasions, the armies assembled by the major nobles – known as barons in England – were stronger than those of their king, who was completely dependent on his aristocrats' loyalty to raise any military contingent and thus was quite weak from a political point of view. To maintain his power, a monarch also had to deal with the interests of the Church

Knight from the First Crusade. The kind of helmet shown in this reconstruction was quite common to find in the lands of the Holy Roman Empire. (*Photo and copyright by Sericum et ferrum*)

Knight from the First Crusade. The helmet shaped like a Phrygian cap was popular among the Norman knights from southern Italy. (*Photo and copyright by Les Seigneurs d'Orient*)

in his own realm. The clergy, in fact, owned significant land properties and fiefdoms in each kingdom and could employ 'moral suasion' to ignite rebellions among commoners.

In 1096, at the beginning of the First Crusade, the Kingdom of England was ruled by the Norman dynasty initiated by William the Conqueror, who in 1066 had left his Duchy of Normandy to claim the English throne. This meant that the English monarch also exerted control over one of the major French fiefdoms – the Duchy of Normandy – and was a vassal of the King of France. Wales, Scotland and Ireland were all still completely independent from England, which was not yet the prominent political power of the British Isles. The French monarchy of the Capetians than the rulers of Norman England. Indeed, the French kings exerted some form of direct control only over a very limited portion of their country, centred on the expanding city of Paris. All the rest of the realm was ruled by warlike aristocrats, who frequently fought against each other and showed only marginal formal respect to royal authority. By the time of the First Crusade, the territories of present-day Germany were organized as the Holy Roman Empire, the direct heir of the Christian empire created a couple of centuries before by Charlemagne. It consisted of a myriad of fully independent feudal princedoms, which were part of the same state only on paper. German emperors had the same basic problems as the English and French kings, but experienced them on a larger scale since their aristocrats were not vassals who had received land properties from them but members of powerful noble families with hereditary rights over their possessions. The clergy in the Holy Roman Empire was extremely rich and influential, to the point that the appointment of a single bishop could determine the destiny of an emperor.

In 1073, Gregory VII became the new Pope, after having been acclaimed by the population of Rome. He had a very precise programme for the reform of the Church, which was designed to reach one main objective: making the clergy fully autonomous from any form of lay political power. Gregory particularly wanted to free the Church from the influence of the Holy Roman Emperors, who, at least on paper, were the overlords of the Italian peninsula and the protectors of the Pope since the days of Charlemagne. In reality, however, most of northern and central Italy was already fully independent from imperial control: the countryside was dominated by autonomous feudal lords, while the major urban centres were developing their own forms of self-government as free *comuni*. In central Italy, there were also lands controlled directly by the Papacy, which had started to form an autonomous state almost three centuries before. The real military protectors of the Pope, since 1054, were the Normans who had settled in southern Italy. Before their arrival, possession of this region had long been contested by the Byzantines and the Lombards. Thanks to their superior military organization, based on the feudal model, the Norman adventurers of the warlike Hauteville family had finally been able to create their own independent realm in the centre of the Mediterranean. After an initial clash, which ended with the defeat of the Papacy at the Battle of Civitate in 1053, the Normans of southern Italy became the main defenders of the Pope and his most important allies in the struggle against the Arab emirate that controlled the island of Sicily. It should be noted that at the beginning of the First Crusade, Sicily – which later became an important base for the Crusaders – was still under Muslim control. At the beginning of the eleventh century, the commercial routes that crossed the Mediterranean were controlled by four Italian port cities, commonly known as the *repubbliche marinare*: Amalfi, Pisa, Genoa and Venice. These cities, being organized as free *comuni*, had large fleets of merchant ships that exported and imported goods from every corner of the Mediterranean. When the Normans conquered southern Italy, the city of Amalfi was destroyed by the invaders, with the decisive support of Pisa. Consequently, during the era of the Crusades, only three *repubbliche marinare* remained active. These were greatly interested in trading with the Middle East and

Knight from the First Crusade, equipped with hauberk of chainmail. (*Photo and copyright by Sericum et ferrum*)

6   Armies of the Crusaders, 1096–1291

French knight from the First Crusade, wearing nasal helmet. (*Photo and copyright by Les Seigneurs d'Orient*)

hoped that new markets could be opened for them in the Levant. As a result, they became one of the main driving forces behind the launching of the Crusades, being the only political entities in Europe with the naval resources needed for transporting large military contingents from Europe to the Middle East.

Christian faith was absolutely dominant in Western Europe by the beginning of the First Crusade. All the commoners living in the various states were true believers, and the monarchs also had to respect the decisions taken by the Papacy. Indeed, the Papacy was a true political power. The Church, differently from the feudal monarchies, had a highly centralized organization that was structured according to rigid hierarchical principles; this was distributed in a methodical way throughout Western Europe and collected taxes for the Papacy from every corner of the Christian world. As a result, through his bishops, the Pope could determine the success or failure of a monarch ruling a distant country. The clergy exerted a strong influence over the commoners, since religion was a fundamental component of the peasants' daily life. For a commoner, loyalty towards the Church could be as important as that towards his king. If excommunicated by the Pope, a monarch could be removed by his subjects, since Divine Law was considered to be superior to Human Law. The European rulers who suffered most from this situation were the Holy Roman Emperors, who gradually lost their control over Italy due to the political machinations of the Popes. In 1075, Gregory VII promulgated an important document known as the *Dictatus Papae*, according to which every monarch was to respect the decisions taken by the Papacy and to follow the moral indications given him by the Pope. Gregory had one main objective in mind: reducing the power of the Holy Roman Emperors by depriving their status of any 'holy' nature, thereby freeing the Church from any form of imperial control. This policy led to the outbreak of an unprecedented clash between Church and Empire in the decades that preceded the First Crusade. From 1075–85, the Holy Roman Emperor Henry IV and Pope Gregory VII were locked in a fierce confrontation. Henry was excommunicated because of his attempts to stop the Gregorian Reform initiated by the *Dictatus Papae*, and in consequence was forced to face several major rebellions launched by the princes of his own state. Having no other choice if he wanted to retain his throne, he was forced to accept humiliating peace conditions and had to beg for the pardon of the Pope. In 1084, having restored his control over Germany, Henry IV entered Italy at the head of an army and took his revenge on Gregory by occupying the city of Rome. The Normans of southern Italy, however, soon came to the aid of the Church and reconquered the city. With the death of Gregory VII in 1085, the clash between Papacy and Empire temporarily came to an end, but some important questions remained unanswered. Only in 1122, with the signing of the Concordat of Worms, were the unsettled problems finally

German knight from the First Crusade. (*Photo and copyright by Sericum et ferrum*)

Norman knight from the First Crusade. In the background is a trebuchet, one of the many siege weapons employed by the Crusaders. (*Photo and copyright by Les Seigneurs d'Orient*)

resolved with a compromise: the bishops of Italy would be chosen by the Pope, while those of Germany would be selected by the Emperor.

Sicily was not the only area of Western Europe where Christians were already fighting against Muslims before the outbreak of the First Crusade. In Spain, the local Christian kingdoms had been trying to expel the Muslims from the Iberian peninsula for several decades. Initially, Arabs from northern Africa had occupied most of the Iberian territories, but with the military intervention of Charlemagne, a significant portion of northern Spain was freed from the Muslims. As a result, some new Christian kingdoms started to emerge in this area. Over time, the kingdoms of Castile and Aragon became the most prominent, especially after the previously dominant Kingdom of León was unified with that of Castile in 1072. All the Christian monarchs of the Iberian peninsula, despite being frequently at war with each other, had one objective in common: expelling the Muslims from their homeland and reconquering Spain and Portugal. The long process of Christian reconquest, known as the *Reconquista*, lasted for centuries and took place simultaneously with the Crusades. In the years preceding the beginning of the First Crusade, the struggle to reclaim Spain had as its main protagonist Rodrigo Díaz de Bivar, the famous warlord known as El Cid. He was able to obtain a series of important victories over the Muslims, including the capture of Valencia in 1094. The *Reconquista* had a lot in common with the Crusades from a practical and ideological point of view; it formally ended only in 1492, when the last Muslims were expelled from southern Spain by forces under Ferdinand II and Isabella I.

The Mediterranean portion of Eastern Europe was dominated by the Byzantine Empire, which was the direct heir of the Roman Empire. From a cultural and social point of view, the *Romaioi* – or Byzantines – were completely different from the rest of Europe: they spoke Greek and were Orthodox Christians, two crucial elements of their civilization. In 1053, after centuries of rising tension between the Pope of Rome and the Patriarch of Constantinople, the Church of Eastern Europe decided to separate from that of Western Europe in what became known as the Great Schism. The new Orthodox Church, guided by the Patriarch of Constantinople and being completely independent from Rome, soon became the most loyal ally of the Byzantine state. The Byzantines had been at war with the Arabs for centuries. Before the ascendancy of the Prophet Muhammad, the Byzantine Empire controlled not only the Balkans but also some portions of southern Italy and vast areas of the Middle East, as well as Egypt. The expansionism of the Muslim Arabs, however, almost caused the collapse of the Byzantine state, as within a short period most of the Byzantine territories located outside the Balkans were conquered. The rich provinces of Syria and Egypt were permanently occupied by the Arabs, who created their own empire in the Mediterranean. After this first phase of Arab expansion, which also saw the fall of Byzantine Palestine – and with it Jerusalem – the Byzantines and Arabs fought for control of the vast Anatolian peninsula (modern-day Turkey). During the last decades of the tenth century, however, a new protagonist arrived on the political scene of the Middle East: the Seljuk Turks. These were a nomadic people of the Eurasian steppes, who had converted to Islam during their migrations across Central Asia. After reaching the Middle East, the Seljuks were able to obtain a series of

Knight from the Second Crusade, wearing mask helmet. (*Photo and copyright by Sericum et ferrum*)

French knight from the Third Crusade, wearing mask helmet. (*Photo and copyright by Les Seigneurs d'Orient*)

victories over both the Byzantines and the Arabs thanks to their military superiority. (The Seljuk armies mostly consisted of mounted archers equipped with the deadly composite bow of the Eurasian peoples.) In 1071, a Byzantine army was destroyed by the Turks at the decisive Battle of Manzikert, which was the greatest disaster in the military history of Byzantium. Following this clash, Anatolia was conquered by the Seljuks and the Byzantines thus lost their last Asian territories. Taking advantage of Byzantium's military weakness, the Normans expelled the last Byzantine troops from southern Italy in 1071, and within a few years – between 1078 and 1083 – they temporarily invaded the Balkan heartland of the Byzantine Empire. By 1096, the

Byzantine state was extremely weak and seemed on the verge of collapse; despite having a flourishing economy and a superior culture, the Empire was weak militarily.

The arrival of the Seljuk Turks also had a devastating impact on the Arab political entities in the Middle East. Until 756, the immense empire conquered by the Arabs remained united as the Abbasid Caliphate; in that year, however, the territories of Muslim Iberia proclaimed their independence and organized themselves as an autonomous emirate. During the following decades, an increasing number of peripheral territories, located far away from the city of Baghdad that was the capital of the Abbasid Caliphate, seceded from the central power. In northern Africa, a local dynasty with its main base in Cairo, the Fatimids, rose to prominence and expelled the Abbasid troops from its territory. The Fatimids slowly expanded throughout the Middle East, conquering Palestine and Syria from the Abbasids, who were left in control of only Iraq. When the Seljuk Turks established bases in Iran in view of their invasion of the Middle East, they learned that the region was still shattered by the internal political divisions of the Arabs. The Fatimids controlled a vast empire and had significant military resources, but they could not resist a mass migration of Turks, having consumed their resources by fighting for decades against the Byzantines, both on land and at sea. After defeating both the Byzantines and the Fatimids, the Turks created their own empire in the Middle East, under the control of Sultan Malik-Shah. When he died in 1092, the new Seljuk state collapsed and entered into a phase of civil wars. The Anatolian territories of the Turks were organized as the Sultanate of Rum, while those in Syria made up a separate state. In 1095, Syria was divided into two rival emirates, one centred around Aleppo and the other on Damascus. As a result of these moves, when the Crusaders invaded the Middle East in 1096, they found the Muslims of the region divided among various opposing states: the Seljuk Sultanate of Rum in Anatolia, the Seljuk Emirate of Aleppo in northern Syria, the Seljuk Emirate of Damascus in southern Syria, the Abbasid Caliphate in Iraq and the Fatimid Caliphate in Egypt and Palestine.

Chapter 2

The First Crusade

In 1095, the energetic Pope Urban II spent several months travelling across Italy and France in order to reassert the authority of the Papacy after the intricate political events that had played out under Pope Gregory VII and Emperor Henry IV. Urban II wanted to carry on the Gregorian Reform and had an ambitious agenda, the main objective of which was achieving the reunification of the Eastern Church with that in the West. In March 1095, a council of ecclesiastics and laymen of the Roman Catholic Church took place at Piacenza, where the Pope met ambassadors sent by the Byzantine Emperor Alexius I Comnenus who described to the synodal assembly the situation, which their state found itself in. The Byzantine envoys explained to the most important members of the Western Church that the Seljuks were in the process of invading the southern Balkans from Anatolia, menacing the imperial city of Byzantium. They feared the arrival of the Turks would be accompanied by vast massacres of Christian civilians, as had already happened in Anatolia after the Battle of Manzikert. Due to their military weakness, caused by the long wars fought against both the Fatimids and the Normans, the Byzantines were in no condition to organize an effective resistance against the Seljuks. In consequence, having no viable alternative, Alexius I had decided to ask for help from Western Europe, where he hoped that the local Christians would decide to assist him by sending troops. The Byzantine Emperor had been excommunicated by Gregory VII several years before, but his relationship with the new Pope Urban II had been generally good since the latter became pontifex in 1088. Urban II hoped that by helping the Byzantines militarily he could finally secure the reunification of the Western and Eastern Church, thereby ending the fracture caused by the Great Schism. After having been intimately informed of the difficult situation that the Byzantine Empire was facing, the Pope decided to organize a new council in France during which he would ask the local aristocracy to assemble a military expedition for the defence of Byzantine lands. The new council took place at Clermont, in central France, in November 1097. The Kingdom of France was the country in medieval Western Europe with the highest number of warlike nobles and knights, who, especially during the eleventh century, spent most of their time fighting against each other and thus had a very violent lifestyle. They lived in massive castles and showed very little respect for the royal authority of their monarch, nor for that of the Church. They treated commoners in a very harsh way and were interested only in plundering the lands of their enemies. Urban II recognized that these warlike feudal warlords represented a great military resource for the Christian world, since they were skilled warriors who loved fighting; all the French aristocrats needed was a 'holy' cause to fight for, possibly far away from their homelands, that had already been devastated by too many feudal wars. Religious zeal was strong among the French knights, most of whom were true believers. Many of them feared that their violent lifestyle could have led their souls to damnation after death, and thus were in search of a way to purify themselves of their many sins. At Clermont, in front of the most important aristocrats of France, Urban II proclaimed the Truce of God, an official decree by the Church that prohibited fighting among feudal lords for a specific period of time. After doing this, the Pope invited the warlike nobles to turn their attentions and energies away from feudal conflicts in order to defend the survival of their faith in other areas. He described how the Seljuk Turks had invaded Byzantine Anatolia and reached the Mediterranean, becoming a serious menace for the Christian world. The nomads of the steppes had killed or enslaved thousands of Christian civilians, devastating religious sites and slaughtering many members of the clergy. After having impressed his audience with his vibrant words, Urban II issued a call to arms: all Christian people of whatever social condition – whether nobles or commoners – were asked to go to the aid of their Christian brothers in the Byzantine Empire. The ensuing conflict, according to the Pope's words, would be a holy war, its main objective being not only simply defending the Byzantine Empire but reconquering Byzantine lands taken by the Muslims during the previous centuries.

In practice, Urban II proposed to organize a massive military expedition directed against the Holy Land for the reconquest of Jerusalem. The Pope promised immediate absolution from all sins to all those who died on the way to the Holy Land or in battle against the Muslims. His political plan was extremely clear: he wanted to channel the bellicosity of the Christian knights towards a holy cause, in order to exert a renewed influence over the Christians of Eastern Europe. Private warfare taking place between feudal lords was a plague for a country like France, so Urban was sure that his unexpected initiative would be well received by the Capetians. By promising an eternal reward to those knights and commoners who marched to the Holy Land, the Pope was sure that it would be possible to assemble a huge military force. However, the Byzantine envoys who had been sent to Piacenza a few months before had not been asking for this. Alexius I had actually only hoped that the Pope could send him some mercenaries recruited from Western Europe, not an entire army of Franks moved by religious zeal. The response of the nobles who were present

Crusader heavy infantryman equipped with hauberk of chainmail. (*Photo and copyright by Les Seigneurs d'Orient*)

Crusader heavy infantryman with kite shield. (*Photo and copyright by Les Seigneurs d'Orient*)

at Clermont to Urban II's call to arms was spontaneous and enthusiastic: they are reported to have cried '*Deus vult*' ('God wills it') in front of the Pope, expressing their will to leave their homeland for the glory of religion. They soon became known as Crusaders, from the Latin words *cruce signati* ('bearers of the cross'), since they started to wear crosses on their clothes and armour as a mark of distinction. Urban II hoped that the knights and commoners would fight together against the common enemy represented by the Muslims, forming a single Christian army that would reach Byzantium. In the end, however, this did not happen, since two different expeditions were organized: one, conducted by commoners, was known as the People's Crusade. while another, consisting of the most important knights of Western Europe, became known as the Princes' Crusade. The two expeditions are collectively known as the First Crusade.

The People's Crusade was organized without the official permission of the Papacy by a charismatic monk and powerful orator named Peter the Hermit, who came from the French city of Amiens. Peter was well known in every corner of France for travelling around the countryside on a donkey and dressing in simple clothing. He was a true predicator, a poor monk who lived among the peasants and experienced their humble way of life. Peter preached the crusade throughout northern France and Flanders, claiming to have been appointed to do so by Christ himself. The charismatic hermit eventually assembled a large number of peasants and low-ranking knights into a giant band of illiterate pilgrims, who had no idea of how to reach the Holy Land but decided to launch a crusade on their own. As the peasants living in northern France and Flanders had been afflicted by drought and famine for many years before 1096, they envisaged Peter's crusade as an opportunity to escape from the hardships of their daily life. Being very superstitious, they were also influenced in their decision to go to the Holy Land by a series of natural events that were perceived as a divine blessing for their movement. During the last weeks of 1095, for example, a lunar eclipse and the passing of a comet took place. Around 100,000 people, including women and children, were under Peter's orders when the People's Crusade began in the summer of 1096. Moving along the Rhine, they destroyed most of the Jewish communities encountered along the way in a series of unprecedentedly large pogroms. Thousands of Jews, who lived and prospered in the Rhineland since centuries, were killed without reason or were forced to become Christians. The worst massacres took place in Worms and Mainz. The religious zeal of the Crusaders made them consider the Jews as enemies of the true religion because – centuries before – their ancestors had killed Christ. After reaching the major city of Cologne on 12 April 1096, Peter gathered his army and remained in Germany in order to gather more supporters from the local peasant communities. Some of his French followers, however, continued the march and crossed from the Holy Roman Empire into the Kingdom of Hungary. The Hungarians controlled a vast portion of the northern Balkans between Germany and the Byzantine Empire. When this group reached the Byzantine border at Belgrade, under the leadership of Walter Sans Avoir, the local authorities temporarily denied them permission to enter Byzantine territory.

After having enlarged his army with many German commoners, Peter continued his march to the Danube, where his forces were split in two: a portion of them decided to continue down the river by boat, but most of them preferred moving overland and thus entered Hungarian territory. In Zemun, not far from the border with the Byzantine Empire, a serious incident took place between the newly arrived Crusaders and the local Hungarian population, which led to the storming of the city and the killing of over 4,000 Hungarians, mostly civilians. The commoners then moved on Belgrade, which was evacuated by the Byzantines in order to avoid further massacres. The city was pillaged and burned by the Crusaders, who continued their march across Byzantine territory. The armed pilgrims from Western Europe were more violent and destructive than an invading army, raiding the countryside in search of supplies and killing everyone who tried to stop them. The Byzantine military authorities were forced to intervene to restore order, attacking the Crusaders and killing almost 10,000 of them. After this clash, the remaining 30,000 armed pilgrims were escorted by Byzantine troops to Byzantium. Alexius I had no idea how to employ this army of peasants that had reached his lands,

Crusader infantryman with padded aketon jacket. (*Photo and copyright by Les Seigneurs d'Orient*)

The First Crusade 19

and feared – correctly – that Peter's men could cause more devastation to his territories. As a result, he quickly ferried them across the Bosporus and left them on the Anatolian coastline. Knowing that most of them had no military capabilities to speak of, he hoped that the Seljuks would soon slaughter them. Once in Anatolia, the commoners began pillaging all the urban settlements that they encountered until they reached Nicomedia. Here, Peter the Hermit completely lost control of his army, since two new leaders were elected: one for the French and another for the Germans. The German commoners, numbering around 6,000, marched on Xerigordos and captured the fortress there. However, they were soon besieged in the stronghold by the Seljuks. The outcome of the siege was decided by the lack of water of those trapped within, who after surrendering were all seized or enslaved by the Turks. The main Crusader army, now consisting of approximately 20,000 French, built a large camp not far from Nicaea, where women and children could rest while the armed men patrolled the surrounding countryside in search of supplies. Three miles from the camp, along a road that entered a narrow and wooded valley, the Seljuks had assembled a large cavalry army consisting of mounted archers. These ambushed the Crusaders and swiftly massacred them with a rain of

Crusader infantryman with nasal helmet. (*Photo and copyright by Les Seigneurs d'Orient*)

Crusader spearman equipped with kite shield. (*Photo and copyright by Les Seigneurs d'Orient*)

Crusader infantryman armed with sword. (*Photo and copyright by Les Seigneurs d'Orient*)

deadly arrows. The camp was soon invested by the Turks, who killed many women and children but spared those who surrendered. The People's Crusade had ended in complete failure due to its complete lack of military organization; having no campaigning experience, it had been seriously damaged by logistical problems and was unable to reach the Holy Land. Only some 3,000 of them survived and were transported back to Byzantium. Clearly, religious zeal was not enough to make a crusade a successful expedition.

Compared with the People's Crusade, which was little more than a disorganized mass pilgrimage, the Princes' Crusade was a well-planned military expedition. Being directed by the Papacy, it started in August 1096 and consisted of four distinct armies that took different routes to Byzantium. According to modern estimates, around 100,000 people participated in the Princes' Crusade: 7,000 knights, 35,000 foot soldiers (mostly feudal peasant levies) and 60,000 civilian non-combatants (including women and children). The spiritual leader of the expedition was Adhemar of Le Puy, one of the most important French bishops, who had been chosen by the Pope because of his military competence and great experience. There were many military leaders among the Princes' Crusade, most of them from the dominant aristocratic families of France: Raymond IV of Toulouse, Godfrey of Bouillon, Baldwin of Boulogne, Hugh of Vermandois, Stephen II of Blois, Robert II of Flanders and Robert Curthouse. Raymond IV, Count of Toulouse, was the most powerful noble of southern France, while Godfrey of Bouillon, Duke of Lower Lorraine, was one of France's most experienced military commanders and had been a loyal supporter of Emperor Henry IV. Baldwin of Boulogne, Count of Verdun, was Godfrey of Bouillon's younger brother, and Hugh of Vermandois, Count of Vermandois, was the younger brother of the King of France, Philip I. Stephen II of Blois, Count of Blois and Chartres, was one of the most powerful aristocrats of northern France and had married William the Conqueror's daughter, Adela of Normandy; Robert II, Count of Flanders, controlled one of Europe's richest regions located between France and Germany; and Robert Curthouse, Duke of Normandy, was the eldest son of William the Conqueror and the older brother of the King of England, William II. In addition to these leaders, there were also two from southern Italy: Bohemond of Taranto and Tancred of Hauteville. Bohemond was the son of Robert Guiscard (the leader of the Norman adventurers who had conquered southern Italy) and was the Prince of Taranto, while Tancred was a nephew of Bohemond and an ambitious young leader. Bohemond of Taranto was a very experienced military commander, having fought under his father's orders when Robert Guiscard tried to invade the Byzantine Empire in 1081. During the latter campaign, at the Battle of Dyrrachium, Bohemond and his father decisively defeated Alexius I and his Byzantine troops. The Norman invasion of the southern Balkans later ended in failure, but the Byzantine Emperor never forgot the defeat that he had suffered at the hands of the Normans from southern Italy. As a result, when Bohemond and Tancred joined the Princes' Crusade, Alexius I became increasingly concerned about the real intentions of the expedition. The Byzantines feared that the Normans had joined the crusade only to pursue their own political interests in an opportunistic way, to invade the southern Balkans.

The main Crusader leaders were major French aristocrats who controlled large territorial possessions in Western Europe, with several of them related to the Norman and Capetian royal families of England and France. Their forces were divided into four separate armies that followed different routes during their journey to the Holy Land. Godfrey of Bouillon and Baldwin of Boulogne crossed the Holy Roman Empire before entering the Kingdom of Hungary, where Baldwin had to be offered as a hostage to King Coloman of Hungary to guarantee the good conduct of Godfrey's troops. The Hungarians had become Christians only during the reign of Stephen I (1000–1038) and did not have a great opinion of the Crusaders, fearing that their realm could be devastated, as had already happened during the People's Crusade. Hughes of Vermandois departed from Paris and crossed France before descending into the Italian peninsula, where he sailed from Apulia across the Adriatic Sea to Dyrrachium. Raymond of Toulouse crossed the Alps and entered northern Italy before marching along the coastline of the western Balkans (present-day Croatia) before reaching the port city of Dyrrachium. Bohemond of Taranto and Tancred of Hauteville assembled their forces in Apulia and then crossed the Adriatic. After disembarking on Byzantine territory, they advanced further into the heart of the southern Balkans. The four Crusader armies converged on Byzantium, where they expected to receive provisions from Alexius I. In return for food and supplies, Alexius requested the western nobles to swear fealty to him and promise to return to the Byzantine Empire any land recovered from the Seljuks. Thereafter, the Crusaders were ferried across the Bosporus by the ships of the Byzantine navy.

After entering Turkish territory, the Crusaders marched across Anatolia without encountering serious opposition. Their first target was the city of Nicaea, the capital of the Seljuk Sultanate of Rum. The Nicaeans had already defeated the People's Crusade and did not expect the arrival of another European expedition; their monarch, Arslan, was campaigning against local enemies in central Anatolia and was not ready to stop the advance of the Crusaders. The Crusaders besieged Nicaea with all their forces, intending to take the city in order to transform it into their main logistical base in Anatolia. Arslan, having been informed of the attack against his capital, assembled all the troops that were at his disposal and advanced towards Nicaea. On 16 May 1097, this Turkish relief force attacked the Crusaders, but was

Crusader sergeant wearing *chapel de fer* helmet.
(*Photo and copyright by Les Seigneurs d'Orient*)

Crusader infantryman armed with axe.
(*Photo and copyright by Les Seigneurs d'Orient*)

defeated during a bloody night battle. Both sides suffered severe losses, but in the end the Seljuk army had no choice but to leave Nicaea to its destiny. After this clash, some Byzantine troops joined the besieging Crusaders. Alexius I now feared that the westerners, after conquering Nicaea, would keep it for themselves. Following the arrival of the Byzantine soldiers, the defenders of Nicaea, being in a desperate situation, finally decided to surrender. However, they gave the city to the commander of the Byzantine troops and not to any of the Crusader leaders. This angered most of the Crusaders, as the Byzantines forbade them from entering Nicaea in groups larger than ten men at a time. Tensions started to grow between the westerners and the Byzantines, especially because the former had suffered significant losses in order to seize the city. Alexius I gave the Crusaders money and rich gifts, hoping that this would be enough to placate their indignation. Eight days after Nicaea fell on 18 June, the Crusaders left to continue their 'liberation' of the Middle East from Muslim rule. They resumed their march in two contingents: one, comprising some Byzantine troops, was commanded by Bohemond and formed the vanguard; the other, consisting of the best French troops, was led by Godfrey and formed the rearguard. While the Crusaders reorganized themselves after the conquest of Nicaea, Arslan gathered a new and much larger army from his Seljuks. He started to closely follow the movements of the Crusaders' vanguard, waiting for the right opportunity to ambush it.

This came on 1 July, outside the urban settlement of Dorylaeum, where Bohemond's Norman and Byzantine troops were surrounded by the Turks and attacked while in their recently built camp. Their leaders had agreed that upon reaching Dorylaeum, the vanguard would stop and wait for the arrival of the rearguard. Initially, Bohemond's Normans suffered significant casualties, coming under a rain of arrows, but they soon mounted their horses and launched counter-attacks against the fast-moving Seljuk cavalry archers. The Seljuks, however, were much faster than the heavy-armoured knights, and were able to escape interception. The Turks then began riding into the enemy camp, cutting down large numbers of non-combatants and foot soldiers, who were unable to deploy in battle formation. At this point, to protect his infantrymen and civilians, Bohemond ordered his knights to dismount and form a defensive line. The footmen and non-combatants were gathered into the centre of the camp, where they tried to support the *milites* as much as possible. The Seljuks attacked the Crusaders' defensive positions in their traditional style, charging in and shooting volleys of arrows before quickly retreating. Being on foot, the Norman knights were unable to to mounts effective counter-attacks, and were obliged to play a passive tactical role. The Turkish arrows did little damage to the heavily armoured knights, but inflicted serious casualties to their horses (which were kept in the centre of the defensive formation). Finding himself in an increasingly difficult situation, Bohemond sent messengers to the rearguard commanded by Godfrey and tried to resist for as long as possible. He was forced back to the banks of the Thymbris River, where the marshy terrain obliged the Seljuks to slow down their assaults. The knights formed a circle around the foot soldiers and civilians, but small groups of them occasionally broke ranks and charged the enemy, only to be slaughtered by the Turks. The Seljuks were surprised by the strength of their opponents' armour, but controlled the battlefield and could move across it unhindered since the Crusaders had no missile troops with which to respond to the volleys of arrows. Just after midday, with the situation turning desperate for Bohemond, Godfrey's reinforcements started to reach the battlefield in small groups. After seven hours of fighting, Raymond arrived with a substantial number of armoured *milites* and launched a surprise charge against one of the Seljuks' exposed flanks. This allowed the dispersed Crusaders to rally and form a well-organized line of battle. The knights rapidly deployed in offensive formation and launched a general charge against the Turks. All the main Crusader leaders were now on the battlefield and participated in the attack. The Seljuks were shocked by the violence and power of the charge, having never seen feudal cavalry in action before. Hundreds of unarmoured Turkish horse archers were slaughtered, especially after some more reinforcements under Adhemar of Le Puy arrived on the battlefield and attacked the Seljuk camp. Finding themselves surrounded with no more hope of victory, the Turks started to flee. The Battle of Dorylaeum thus, against all odds, resulted in a decisive success for the Crusaders.

At the end of the clash, the victorious Crusaders looted the enemy camp and captured the rich treasury of Arslan. The Seljuk ruler, being in no condition to fight another battle against the invaders, burned and destroyed everything he left behind in his army's flight. He adopted effective scorched earth tactics, which heavily impacted on the Crusaders as it was the middle of summer and they had very few supplies with them in Anatolia. The local population of the region did not consider the Western knights as liberators and did not help them by providing supplies. To keep moving, the extremely numerous Crusader army needed large quantities of water and food, which were not in plentiful supply in the inhospitable lands of southern Anatolia. After passing through the Cilician Gates, a strategic mountain pass that connected southern Anatolia with northern Syria, Baldwin and Tancred decided to break away from the main body of the Crusader army and set off towards Cilician Armenia. This region, also known as Lesser Armenia, was a small state created around 1080 by Armenian refugees who were fleeing the Seljuk invasion of their homeland in the Caucasus (present-day Armenia). Cilician Armenia was located in south-western Anatolia, in an area covered by mountains that was of great strategic importance since it connected Anatolia with Syria and was not distant from the sea. As we have seen, among the Crusader leaders, Baldwin and Tancred were more interested in conquering a region of the Holy Land for themselves in order to become major feudal lords; they, in fact, did not control large possessions in Europe. In Cilician Armenia, the great majority of the local population consisted of Christians, who were ready to support the westerners by providing them with supplies and guides. After defeating the Seljuk garrison of Tarsus, Baldwin and Tancred were welcomed by the Armenian people. At that time, Cilician Armenia was fragmented into a series of minor states controlled by local rulers, who had been at war with the Turks for several years and thus welcomed the arrival of the Crusaders. Some Armenian rulers, however, soon understood that the Crusaders had only come to rest and not just to free them from the Turks. Consequently, the western knights had to fight some minor clashes against groups of Armenians who resisted their arrival. On 10 March 1098, after having occupied a good portion of Cilician Armenia, Baldwin assumed the title of Count of Edessa, establishing the first of the so-called Crusader states of the Middle East. The occupation of the Armenian lands located along the

Crusader archer.
(*Photo and copyright by Les Seigneurs d'Orient*)

Crusader archer firing with his longbow. (*Photo and copyright by Les Seigneurs d'Orient*)

Crusader crossbowman. (*Photo and copyright by Les Seigneurs d'Orient*)

Crusader peasant pilgrim. (*Photo and copyright by Les Seigneurs d'Orient*)

Euphrates River by Baldwin and Tancred secured an important source of supplies for the Crusaders, who finally started to control some territories of the Levant. The lands making up the new County of Edessa, however, were not given back to the Byzantine Empire as promised by the western leaders several months before. Until that moment, thanks to the success of the Crusaders, Alexius I had been able to reconquer a large portion of western Anatolia without employing significant numbers of his troops. Following the Armenian campaign of Baldwin and Tancred, however, the situation started to change as the Crusader warlords began keeping the newly conquered lands for themselves.

While these events took place in Cilician Armenia, the main Crusader army marched on to Antioch, one of the Middle East's most important and richest cities, situated midway between Byzantium and Jerusalem. Being well-fortified and having a large population, it had to be captured by the Crusaders if they wanted to continue their march across Syria. Upon reaching Antioch, the western leaders saw that it would be impossible for them to storm the city since its defences were too strong; as a result, they started besieging Antioch in the hope of forcing it into capitulation without having to suffer serious losses. The siege began on 20 October 1097, but the Crusaders quickly started to experience serious difficulties. First of all, they did not have enough troops to fully surround the large urban centre, which was thus able to remain partially supplied. The army besieged Antioch for eight months without achieving anything. Thousands of Crusaders died of starvation, since the supplies available to them were not sufficient to sustain such a large army operating in a foreign country. Meanwhile, the Seljuk rulers of Aleppo and Damascus, who were two brothers but were at war against each other, sent separate relief armies against the Crusaders that were easily repulsed.

Realizing that the Crusaders were too weak to conquer Antioch, the Turks decided to put aside their political differences and raise a single relief army to be guided by a leader named Kerbogha. The Crusader leaders besieging Antioch spent most of their time quarrelling among themselves, each of them plotting to transform the city into one of his personal domains. Bohemond, in particular, was determined to gain control of Antioch since it was seen as the gateway to Syria. Stephen of Blois left the besieging army during the most difficult moment of the siege and informed Alexius I that the Byzantine cause in the Middle East was lost, since the other Crusader leaders had no intention to free any land for the Byzantines. Alexius I had assembled an army to support the westerners in their siege of Antioch and was marching through Anatolia when he was informed by Stephen about the real intentions of the Crusader leaders. Now hoping that the besiegers would be defeated by the Seljuks, the Byzantine Emperor returned to his capital without sending any reinforcements or supplies to the Crusaders. On 2 June, however, an Armenian traitor living inside Antioch, having been paid by Bohemond, opened a gate of the city and allowed a small party of Crusaders to enter. Seeing this, the Christian inhabitants of Antioch opened the other gates of their city in order to help the Crusaders. After months of suffering near starvation, the army meted out extreme violence upon penetrating the city. They sacked and killed without mercy, also causing significant losses to the Christian civilians of Antioch. The citadel of the city, however, remained in Turkish hands and continued to resist thanks to its strong fortifications. On 4 June, the vanguard of Kerbogha's army of 40,000 men arrived outside Antioch. The Crusaders, taken by surprise, had to hastily improvise a defence of the city. Fortunately for them, however, the walls of Antioch had not been damaged during the siege. From 10 June, Kerbogha's soldiers assaulted Antioch's walls for four days from dawn until dusk. The western forces, despite being heavily outnumbered, managed to hold out. The city gates were barred to prevent desertions and the civilian population was forced to support the Crusaders. After having been repulsed several times, the attackers stopped their assaults and settled down to a siege in the hope of starving out those now trapped in the city. Morale inside Antioch rapidly plummeted, with hundreds of soldiers and civilians dying from starvation. Once again, the Crusaders did not have sufficient supplies with them and had not planned the logistical aspects of their military actions. When everything seemed lost, a peasant visionary who was with the Crusader army – named Peter Bartholomew – claimed that Saint Andrew had shown him the location of the Holy Lance that had pierced Christ on the cross. The Holy Lance was found exactly where Peter Bartholomew searched for it, which boosted the morale of the exhausted defenders. Having no more supplies left but now being full of religious zeal, the Crusaders marched out of Antioch in four groups on 28 June in an attempt to engage the enemy in a decisive – albeit desperate – pitched battle. Kerbogha did not stop the deployment of the enemy army, as he wanted to destroy it as soon as possible and was confident of his soldiers' superiority. Kerbogha's troops, however, did not consist only of Seljuks, also comprising large numbers of non-professional fighters. In consequence, when the Crusaders ventured out from Antioch, the Muslims could only launch a disorderly attack against them. The Crusaders, knowing that their destiny depended on the outcome of the battle, charged against the Muslims with violent desperation, quickly killing hundreds of them. The besieging army of Kerbogha was destroyed, those who survived swiftly fleeing. Seeing these events, the remaining Turkish defenders of the city's citadel finally surrendered. It had been a complete victory for the Crusaders, and especially for Bohemond, who thereafter became the ruler of Antioch. The Norman leader soon argued that Alexius I's decision to abandon them to their destiny had invalidated all

Templar knight with mask helmet. (*Photo and copyright by Ordenskomturei Heppenheim*)

Templar knight with great helmet. (*Photo and copyright by Ordenskomturei Heppenheim*)

the Crusaders' oaths to him, so following the conquest of Antioch, they began to act independently from the Byzantines and the whole enterprise assumed a new nature. The Crusaders were now fighting to conquer the Holy Land for themselves, not to restore the Byzantine presence in the Middle East.

After occupying Antioch, the Crusaders once again began quarrelling among themselves and remained inactive for several months. Now that the expedition had turned into a campaign of conquest, all the various leaders wanted to create their own fiefdom in the Middle East. Furthermore, the three main groups that made up the Crusader army also had contrasting interests in Europe. For instance, the nobles of northern France hated those of southern France and had long planned to invade their lands, while the Norman nobles of southern Italy were considered by the French Crusaders to be no better than pirates who simply wanted to become rich by plundering the Holy Land. While they all discussed how best to continue the campaign, a plague broke out among the ranks of the Crusader army and killed hundreds of people (including Adhemar, who had tried to limit the personal ambitions of the various warlords and to keep the army under the direct control of the Pope). The Crusader forces were in no condition to continue their march across the Middle East after having stopped in Antioch for so many months; they had very few horses and – as usual – suffered from a chronic lack of supplies. The Muslim peasants living in the countryside around Antioch refused to give them food, and all the nearby areas had already been pillaged during the previous months. Once again being on the verge of starvation at the beginning of 1099, they had no choice but to resume their advance towards the heart of the Holy Land. Many knights and commoners were becoming impatient and seemed ready to revolt against their leaders. Meanwhile, the lengthy delay at Antioch by the Crusaders had worked in favour of the Muslims, who had been able to improve their defences. When the Crusader army finally left Antioch, Bohemond remained in the city as the first Prince of Antioch. The new Crusader state created by Bohemond, the Principality of Antioch, later became a flourishing one. In order to receive enough supplies by sea, the Crusader army resumed its advance by moving along the Mediterranean coast of the Holy Land.

The Crusaders encountered little resistance during this phase of their expedition, the local rulers of the area located between northern Syria and Palestine preferring to make peace with them and to furnish them with supplies rather than seeing their lands devastated. After Bohemond remained in Antioch, the internal hierarchy among the leaders of the western knights changed significantly. Robert Curthouse and Tancred agreed to become vassals of Raymond IV of Toulouse in the hope of receiving some lands from him in the Holy Land in exchange for their military services. Raymond was by then the strongest and wealthiest of the Crusader leaders marching across the Levant. Tancred had tried to obtain some lands in Cilician Armenia, but without success; he had then attempted to become Bohemond's right arm in Antioch, but ultimately did not receive the political power that he so strongly desired. As a result, the ambitious Norman noble allied himself with his former rival, Raymond, who hated his uncle Bohemond. Godfrey of Bouillon, now counting on the support of his brother who had become Prince of Edessa, emerged as the alternative leader to Raymond. Nevertheless, during the march towards Jerusalem, Raymond decided to take the important city of Tripoli in order to transform it into the capital of a new Crusader state to be created north of Palestine. To achieve his objective, however, he first had to besiege the fortified city of Arqa in northern Lebanon. While Raymond was fighting at Arqa, Godfrey and Robert of Flanders continued their march southwards in the hope of reaching Jerusalem first. Tancred, who had been loyal to Raymond until that moment, decided to follow Godfrey and Robert after he discovered that the new Crusader state to be created in Tripoli would never be assigned to him. However, Raymond's siege of Arqa was a complete failure, the city remaining unconquered. Tension was now growing among the Crusader leaders due to their internal rivalries, and thus any military setback – even if only temporary – risked provoking the collapse of the whole expedition.

Following Adhemar's death, there had been no real spiritual leader of the Crusade. The discovery of the Holy Lance had not resolved this problem, as there had been public accusations of fraud among the opposing clerical factions that participated in the expedition. Peter Bartholomew, the man who had discovered the relic, was challenged to an ordeal by fire; he underwent it and died after days of terrible agony from his wounds. This discredited the Holy Lance as a fake and also undermined Raymond's political authority, since he had been one of the main proponents of its authenticity. While these events took place among the Crusaders, a new conflict broke out among the Muslims. Shortly before the arrival of the invaders in Anatolia, Jerusalem and most of Palestine had been occupied by the Seljuks, who temporarily defeated the local Fatimid garrisons. After the Crusaders crushed most of the Turks' military power, however, the Fatimids took advantage of the situation to launch a campaign of reconquest in Palestine from their Egyptian territories. A few months before the arrival of the Crusaders in front of its walls, the Holy City of Jerusalem was reoccupied by the Fatimids, who expelled the Seljuks from most of Palestine. The Fatimids, after obtaining this success, tried to make a deal with the Crusaders by promising freedom of passage to any pilgrim directed to the Holy Land in exchange for their promise to not invade Fatimid lands. The offer, however, was promptly refused by the Crusaders, who were by now strongly convinced that it would be quite easy to conquer Jerusalem. The city had a new Fatimid governor, named Iftikhar

Templar knight armed with spear and mace. (*Photo and copyright by Ordenskomturei Heppenheim*)

Templar knight wearing the cloak of his religious order. (*Photo and copyright by Ordenskomturei Heppenheim*)

ad-Daula, who became increasingly worried about the imminent arrival of the Crusaders and thus decided to expel all the Christian inhabitants from Jerusalem, fearing that they could have helped the western knights during an eventual siege. The Fatimid commander knew that the military forces under his direct control were too small to confront the invaders in a pitched battle, and had been impressed by the accounts of the previous clashes between the Crusaders – described as 'wild beasts' because of their ferocity in combat – and the Seljuks. As a result of this, Iftikhar ad-Daula prepared his troops for a long siege. His plan was a very simple one: force the Crusaders to remain blocked outside the walls of Jerusalem for several months, then to run out of supplies and die of starvation. To achieve his objective he reinforced the defences of the Holy City and poisoned most of the wells in the surroundings of Jerusalem. Upon reaching Tripoli, the Crusader leaders were convinced that they would be obliged to fight in order to occupy the city. However, contrary to their expectations, the governor of the city surrendered without a fight. He provided the Crusaders with many fine horses and promised that he would convert to Christianity if they defeated his Fatimid enemies.

The Crusaders advanced rapidly towards Palestine in the spring of 1099: on 19 May they passed Beirut and on 23 May Tyre, without meeting opposition from the local troops. They thus entered Palestine without any fighting, reaching the city of Ramla, which had been hastily abandoned by its inhabitants. Ramla was soon transformed into their main base by the Crusader leaders, who started planning their next move, having as their main objective freeing those area of Palestine where Jesus Christ was said to have lived. On 6 June, Godfrey sent Tancred with a token force to Bethlehem, which they easily occupied without suffering any losses. Tancred had the great personal satisfaction of placing his banner over the Church of the Nativity, one of the most important Christian sites of the Holy Land. On 7 June, after a short march, the main Crusader army arrived in view of Jerusalem; for many of the force, this was a dream coming true, a moment of their lives that they would never forget. The Fatimids, however, were expecting them and had prepared themselves for a long siege. Additional supplies had been stored inside Jerusalem, an elite force of 400 cavalry from Egypt had reinforced the local garrison and all the trees located around the Holy City had been cut down. The latter move was a very intelligent one: to build the siege machines needed to assault Jerusalem, the Crusaders would now be obliged to search for large amounts of wood far from the besieged city, which would cause them serious delays. Jerusalem was guarded by a defensive wall stretching for 4km, and was 3m thick and 15m high. Such defences, by the standards of the time, were very impressive. Five major gates opened in the walls, each of which was protected by a pair of towers. The Crusaders, soon after starting the siege, divided their forces

Templar knight with great helmet. (*Photo and copyright by Ordenskomturei Heppenheim*)

42 Armies of the Crusaders, 1096–1291

Templar knight armed with sword and mace. (*Photo and copyright by Ordenskomturei Heppenheim*)

in two: one part, commanded by Godfrey, camped in front of Jerusalem's northern side, while the other, under Raymond, camped on the Holy City's southern side. By attacking from two sides at the same time, they hoped to more easily overcome the defenders.

The Crusaders launched their first frontal assault on 13 June, but as they had no access to wood for the construction of siege equipment they attacked Jerusalem's walls with the single ladder they had been able to build. Such logistical unpreparedness was a perfect example of the many improvisations that the Crusaders had to make during an expedition that had been more successful than expected. By attacking with just one ladder at a single point of the walls, they had no hope of success. They did fight with great courage during the assault and one of them – a knight named Rainbold – even managed to scale the ladder and gain a foothold on the walls, but in the end the attack was repulsed with significant losses. Religious zeal was not enough to take a well-fortified city like Jerusalem. Demoralized but not defeated, the Crusaders retreated to their lines and decided to not launch any new assault until they found enough wood to build proper siege machines and many ladders. Indeed, without at least two siege towers it would have been impossible to attack the city from the north and the south at the same moment. In this phase of the siege, the Christian forces faced many difficulties, including lack of water and shortages of food, the latter the result of the Fatimids' scorched earth tactics. The summer temperatures in Palestine did not help the besiegers, who were not used to such heath. By the end of June, the Crusader leaders learnt that a powerful Fatimid relief force was entering southern Palestine from Egypt. They realized they had to act quickly in order to take Jerusalem before the arrival of the enemy army. The besiegers were in a very difficult strategic situation: they were camped in an arid countryside, where no natural resources were available, and furthermore there was no hope of them trying to blockade Jerusalem as they had with Antioch because the Holy City was too large. Previous clashes during the expedition, together with desertions, had greatly reduced the strength of the Crusaders, who by now numbered some 12,000 men, of whom only 1,500 were knights. On 17 June, with the Crusader army seeming to be on the verge of annihilation, relief came with the arrival in the port of Jaffa of some Genoese ships under the command of Guglielmo Embriaco. The Genoese sailors came to the aid of the Crusaders at the most decisive moment of the campaign, providing them with skilled engineers capable of building effective siege machines as well as with large amounts of timber (stripped from the ships, which were hauled ashore). After the arrival of the Genoese vessels, the besiegers' morale was further raised by a priest named Peter Desiderius, who claimed to have had a vision of Adhemar of Le Puy during which the Crusaders were instructed to march barefoot in procession around Jerusalem's walls, after which the city would fall (as had happened during the Biblical episode of the siege of Jericho). On 8 July, the Crusaders duly performed the procession exactly as they had been instructed by Peter Desiderius, ending on the Mount of Olives where the various factions existing among the besiegers finally came together in public unity.

Within three weeks of the Genoese ships arriving, the Crusaders had built some of the most effective siege equipment ever employed during the eleventh century. This included two massive wheel-mounted siege towers, a battering ram with an iron-clad head, several scaling ladders and numerous portable wattle screens. The attackers had to defend themselves from the arrows of the enemy and needed two siege towers in order to attack Jerusalem from different points at the same time. The Fatimids were fearful when they saw the siege equipment arranged against them, but were ready to respond with their mangonel catapults mounted on the walls. The final assault on Jerusalem began on 13 July. Raymond's troops, attacking from the south, made little progress and suffered severe losses, but Godfrey's men, attacking from the north, soon started to push – slowly but steadily – the Fatimid defenders away from the walls. At the end of the first day of fighting, however, the battlements were still in Muslim hands. On 15 July the Crusaders resumed their attack with increasing determination, having understood that the Fatimid troops were already weakened. After a violent struggle, the inner rampart of the northern wall was finally occupied by Godfrey's knights. Upon this, the Fatimid soldiers panicked and abandoned all of Jerusalem's northern walls. The Crusaders entered the city and started to massacre all the Muslim and Jewish civilians they encountered, showing no mercy. The Fatimid troops fled to the Temple Mount, with Tancred and his knights in close pursuit. The Norman leader reached the Temple Mount before the defenders could establish a new defensive position, and his men slaughtered many of the surviving Fatimids. The few survivors took refuge in the Al-Aqsa Mosque, being determined to fight to the last man. At this point, however, Tancred called a halt to his attack and offered his personal protection to the Fatimids in the mosque in exchange for their immediate surrender. While these events took place in the northern part of Jerusalem, to the south the Fatimid troops continued to resist the attacks of Raymond until they were informed that the northern wall had fallen. Thereupon, they left their positions and retreated to the Holy City's citadel, allowing Raymond to enter Jerusalem. Iftikhar ad-Daula, seeing that his situation was hopeless, decided to make a deal with Raymond, surrendering the citadel in return for being granted safe passage to Ascalon. After the last Fatimid troops gave up the fight, the slaughter of civilians continued for the rest of the day. Thousands of Muslims – including many women and children – were victims of the fury of the Chrstian soldiers. Many Jews, who had taken refuge in their synagogue, were killed when the building was burnt down by the Crusaders. On the following day, Tancred's prisoners who had surrendered in the Al-Aqsa Mosque were also massacred. The few Muslims and Jews who were not killed by the Crusaders hastily left Jerusalem or were taken prisoner to be ransomed.

Templar sergeant with mask helmet. (*Photo and copyright by Ordenskomturei Heppenheim*)

Templar sergeant. (*Photo and copyright by Ordenskomturei Heppenheim*)

According to eyewitness accounts, the streets of the Holy City literally ran with blood, with around 40,000 civilians slaughtered.

On 17 July, a council was held among the victorious Crusader leaders to decide who was to be crowned as the new King of Jerusalem. After some lively discussions, Godfrey of Bouillon – whose troops had played a fundamental role during the siege – was named Advocatus Sancti Sepulchri (Defender of the Holy Sepulchre). The experienced warlord refused to be named as king in the city where Jesus Christ had died, showing his respect for religion. Arnulf of Chocques, one of Raymond's most loyal followers, was elected the first Latin Patriarch of Jerusalem on 1 August; four days later, after consulting some surviving inhabitants of the city, he discovered the holy relic of the True Cross. Urban II, the instigator of the First Crusade, died on 29 July 1099, a few days before he could be informed of Jerusalem's recapture. Soon after the western forces consolidated their presence in the Holy City, Fatimid ambassadors arrived in Jerusalem and ordered the Crusaders to leave the city as soon as possible. Godfrey, who had not forgotten that a large enemy army was on its way from Egypt, prepared his remaining forces for the last battle of the expedition. He marched towards Ascalon with most of the other leaders, except for Raymond of Toulouse and Robert of Normandy, who only left Jerusalem the day after the main Crusader army had moved against the enemy. Near Ramla, the Crusaders were joined by Tancred and by Godfrey's brother, Eustace, who had been sent with some knights to capture Nablus after the fall of Jerusalem. The main army, guided by Godfrey, marched with Patriarch Arnulf at its head with the relics of the True Cross and the Holy Lance. The Fatimid army that was invading southern Palestine consisted of 20,000 men, coming from every corner of the Muslim world, and was supported by a fleet anchored in the port of Ascalon. The Fatimid commanders, unaware that the Crusaders were marching against them with their whole army, had planned to besiege Jerusalem and retake it as soon as possible. On 11 August, upon reaching Ascalon, the Christian forces found sheep and goats gathered outside the city to feed the nearby Fatimid camp. According to some captives taken by Tancred near Ramla, the animals had been left free to encourage the Crusaders to disperse for pillaging, which would have given a decisive advantage to the Fatimids. Godfrey, however, maintained order among his troops and captured the cattle without dispersing his forces. On the morning of 12 August, the Crusaders deployed their forces in three main divisions: the left was commanded by Godfrey, with the centre under the orders of Tancred and the right wing led by Raymond, who had by now joined the rest of the Christian forces. Each division consisted of three smaller sub-divisions: one of foot soldiers marching at the front and two of knights in the rear. The decisive clash of the campaign took place not far from Ascalon and from the Fatimid camp. While

Templar sergeant with 'great helmet'. Over the chainmail he is wearing a corselet reinforced with iron plates. (*Photo and copyright by Ordenskomturei Heppenheim*)

Templar sergeant wearing the monastic clothes of his religious order. (*Photo and copyright by Ordenskomturei Heppenheim*)

it did not last for long, it was extremely violent. Initially, the Fatimid vanguard was able to outflank the Crusaders and to surround their rearguard, but this assault was repulsed by Godfrey. During the ensuing hand-to-hand fighting, which involved only a portion of the Muslim troops, the Fatimids suffered severe casualties, their lightly armoured troops proving no match for the veteran Christian *milites*. The Fatimids soon panicked and fled back to the safety of Ascalon's walls, leaving the Crusaders victorious. Tancred captured the Fatimid camp and its treasures, but the city of Ascalon could not be seized by Godfrey due to the presence of a strong garrison as well as the large Egyptian fleet. During the following years, the city would become the main base of operations for all the forces from Egypt that attacked the Crusader Kingdom of Jerusalem.

Chapter 3

The Second Crusade

Following the Battle of Ascalon, most of the Crusaders considered their holy pilgrimage to Palestine was complete and thus returned home. Only 300 knights and 2,000 foot soldiers remained in Jerusalem with Godfrey to garrison the new Crusader state that was in the process of being organized. Most of those who decided to remain were from Godfrey's native Lorraine, which enabled him to secure his secular leadership over Jerusalem, despite Raymond's strong claims. Despite this, there was some uncertainty about what to do with the new Kingdom of Jerusalem. The new papal legate, the energetic Daimbert of Pisa, was chosen as Latin Patriarch of the Holy City and convinced Godfrey to hand over Jerusalem to him, with the intention of setting up a theocratic state that would be placed under direct papal control. The Papacy wanted to create a new Papal State in the Middle East, following the example of that already existing in central Italy. Godfrey accepted Daimbert's proposal, in exchange for the promise of being given other cities – located not far from Jerusalem – as his personal domains in the Holy Land. Consequently, soon after the end of the First Crusade, Godfrey and his men conquered the important Palestinian cities of Jaffa, Haifa and Tiberias. Other urban centres were reduced to the state of vassals. Godfrey soon tried to introduce feudalism in the Kingdom of Jerusalem, compensating his most loyal followers with fiefdoms. It was during this transitional phase that the Principality of Galilee and the County of Jaffa were established as fiefdoms of the Kingdom of Jerusalem. Godfrey of Bouillon's reign over Jerusalem, however, was quite short, since he died of an illness in 1100 just a few months after the end of the First Crusade. His brother, the ambitious Baldwin of Boulogne, took his place. Baldwin had plans that were completely different from those of Godfrey: he refused the idea of giving up the Holy City to papal control and opposed the creation of a theocratic state. He claimed Jerusalem for himself and assumed the title of King of the Latins of Jerusalem, obliging Daimbert to crown him in Bethlehem. Thanks to Baldwin's efforts, the secular Kingdom of Jerusalem was finally established. While these events took place in Palestine, the other Middle Eastern states created by the Crusaders started to organize themselves. Before assuming power in Jerusalem, Baldwin had been the ruler of the County of Edessa in Cilician Armenia, where he was succeeded by his cousin, Baldwin of Bourcq, who soon started work in order to establish positive relations with his new Armenian subjects. Baldwin married an Armenian princess and tried to respect the traditions of the local Christians, consolidating the Crusader presence in Edessa. After becoming Baldwin II, he formed a strong alliance with the Principality of Antioch that had been created by Bohemond during the First Crusade. Bohemond and his Norman followers had not participated to the siege of Jerusalem but had soon started to fight against the Muslims living on the borders of their state. In particular, they had to face the Danishmends, ferocious Turks belonging to an ethnic group that was not part of the Seljuks. Before the First Crusade, the Danishmends had created their own autonomous state in north-eastern Anatolia and had been fighting for a long time against the Seljuks to preserve their independence. In 1100, while campaigning against the Danishmends, Bohemond was captured; as a result, his ambitious nephew, Tancred, became regent of the Principality of Antioch. Tancred – who assumed the title of Prince of Galilee – soon expanded the borders of the state, attacking the Byzantines and taking various important Anatolian cities from them, including Tarsus and Latakia. He also formed a strong military alliance with Baldwin II of Edessa,

Hospitaller sergeant armed with spear. (*Photo and copyright by Ordenskomturei Heppenheim*)

Templar sergeant wearing *chapel de fer* helmet. (*Photo and copyright by Ordenskomturei Heppenheim*)

who wished to expand the borders of his state and thus soon started to attack Seljuk territories located near his County of Edessa. In 1103, Bohemond was released by the Danishmends and quickly went back to his realm in order to support Baldwin II and Tancred in their expansionist efforts. In 1104, the ruler of Edessa attacked and besieged the city of Harran, garrisoned by the Seljuks, where he was soon joined by his allies Bohemond and Tancred, marching from the south.

The Turks responded to these moves by assembling a large army and sending it against Edessa, convinced that Baldwin II would stop his offensive campaign in order to defend his capital. While the Turks were besieging Edessa, however, Bohemond and Tancred arrived from the south, at which the Seljuks decided to abandon the siege and to make a feigned retreat towards Harran. The Crusaders followed them in close pursuit, until the Turkish army stopped a short distance from Harran. Here the Crusader leaders, who had joined their forces, came under a surprise attack from their elusive enemies. The Seljuks suddenly stopped their feigned retreat and attacked their pursuers when they were completely unprepared. Most of the knights were not wearing their armour since they were on the march, and thus could not protect themselves from the enemy arrows. The Crusaders had only a very short time to deploy their troops on the battlefield: Baldwin II and his troops from Edessa were on the left wing, while Bohemond and Tancred were on the right wing with their forces from Antioch. The Battle of Harran ended in disaster for the Crusaders, who were completely routed. Baldwin II was captured together with several of his men, although Bohemond and Tancred were

Templar sergeant armed with pike. (*Photo and copyright by Ordenskomturei Heppenheim*)

Templar sergeant with *chapel de fer* helmet. (*Photo and copyright by Ordenskomturei Heppenheim*)

able to escape to Edessa. Baldwin was eventually freed four years later, in 1108. The clash was the first serious defeat suffered by the westerners in the Middle East since the beginning of the First Crusade. The Byzantine Empire took advantage of it, recapturing the city of Latakia and parts of Cilicia from the Crusaders. Being short of military resources to face the Byzantines, Bohemond went to southern Italy to recruit more Norman troops. In 1107, instead of landing with the reinforcements in the Holy Land, Bohemond decided to cross the Adriatic Sea with a fleet and attack the Byzantines in the southern Balkans. As he had already done in his youth, he laid siege to the important coastal city of Dyrrhachium in an attempt to transform it into his main base in the Balkans. Despite their efforts, however, the Normans were unable to make any significant advance, with Alexius I avoided any pitched battle with his Byzantine troops. Bohemond's siege of Dyrrhachium failed completely after a plague killed many of his soldiers. After these events, the Norman leader was obliged to sign the humiliating Treaty of Devol, according to which the Principality of Antioch was to become a vassal state of the Byzantine Empire upon Bohemond's death.

Meanwhile, in the Holy Land, Tancred had assumed the regency of the County of Edessa following the capture of Baldwin II. Bohemond soon started planning his revenge on Alexius I and after some months spent in Antioch, returned to southern Italy to recruit more Norman troops. While in the Italian peninsula, in 1111, he died. Tancred, who was no longer the regent of Edessa by that time, succeeded him as the ruler of Antioch. Alexius I did his best to oblige Tancred to accept Byzantine overlordship over the Principality of Antioch, but without success. Then in 1112, Tancred also died and was succeeded as ruler of Antioch by Bohemond's son, who became Bohemond II. Raymond of Toulouse, having been unable to become the ruler of Jerusalem, tried to create his own state in the Middle East, angry that minor warlords had established their own realms in Edessa and Antioch while he owned no land in the region. During the course of the First Crusade, as we have seen, Raymond had planned to occupy the major city of Tripoli that was now located between the Crusader states of the north and the larger Kingdom of Jerusalem. During the First Crusade, the governor of Tripoli had been able to preserve the autonomy of his city by surrendering to the Christian knights and supplying them with provisions. Raymond knew very well that Tripoli was surrounded by fertile lands and that by conquering the city, he would be able to control the land routes connecting the Norman territorial possessions in the north with the French ones in the south. As a result, after occupying Tartus, he prepared his forces to attack Tripoli in 1103. The city was well fortified and Raymond had to besiege it for many months before taking his prize. In 1105, however, the Crusader leader died before being able to complete the conquest of Tripoli; the port remained in Muslim hands. After Raymond's death, two rival leaders claimed to be his heir: the first was Raymond's cousin William, Count of Cerdagne, while the second was Raymond's illegitimate son, Bertrand of Toulouse. William was supported by Tancred of Galilee, while Bertrand had the backing of Baldwin I of Jerusalem. To avoid the outbreak of a large-scale conflict among the Crusaders, the succession was resolved with a compromise inspired by Baldwin I. William would rule the northern part of Tripoli and be a vassal of Tancred, whereas Bertrand would reign over the southern part of Tripoli and be a vassal of the King of Jerusalem. After this settlement was accepted by all parts, the Crusaders joined their forces and resumed the siege of Tripoli's fortified port. This was finally taken on 12 July 1109, shortly after which William of Cerdagne was killed (he was probably murdered) and thus Bertrand of Toulouse – strongly supported by the Genoese – remained as the sole ruler of the newly established County of Tripoli.

Under Baldwin I's rule, the Kingdom of Jerusalem had seen a significant territorial expansion, which was made possible by the arrival of more western troops in the Holy Land, especially following a minor expedition that took place in 1101. Following the success of the First Crusade, enthusiasm spread in Western Europe and an increasing number of knights and commoners decided to head for the Holy Land to visit Jerusalem as pilgrims. In September 1100, a large group of Lombard peasants from the surroundings of Milan, guided by that city's bishop, Anselm IV, left Italy for the Middle East. Upon reaching the territory of the Byzantine Empire, they pillaged it with extreme violence. Alexius I, to limit the damage to his lands, promptly escorted the Lombard Crusaders to a large camp outside Byzantium. However, the Crusaders made their way inside the Byzantine capital and pillaged parts of it. After this, they were hastily ferried across the Bosporus and camped in Nicomedia awaiting reinforcements. These came in May 1101 and consisted of a small but strong contingent that was almost entirely composed of knights. These were commanded by some of Western Europe's most prominent nobles, including Eudes I, Duke of Burgundy, and Conrad, the Constable of the Holy Roman Empire. Overall command of the Crusader forces assembling in Nicomedia was assumed by Raymond of Toulouse, who wanted to employ the newcomers in his private army to help him conquer some lands for himself. The Crusaders occupied some minor towns but were harassed by the Seljuks, who attacked them several times with hit-and-run tactics. The inexperienced Lombards then moved east towards the territory of the Danishmends, with the objective of rescuing Bohemond of Taranto who had been captured by them. At this point, the Seljuk ruler of Rum Arslan, who had already been defeated during the First Crusade and feared that his remaining Anatolian domains could be taken by the western knights, decided to form a military alliance with the Danishmends. A large Muslim army was assembled and marched against the Crusaders, resulting in a decisive clash at the Battle of Mersivan, where the Turks destroyed the forces commanded by Raymond. Most of the Lombard peasants, fighting as infantrymen, were slaughtered, and thus the small-scale Crusade of 1101 ended in complete failure.

While these events took place, various other expeditions tried to reach the Holy Land. A force under the command of William II of Nevers arrived in the Holy Land shortly after Raymond's army left Nicomedia. It briefly besieged Konya – without success – before being ambushed at Heraclea Cybistra by the victorious Arslan (who had just won the Battle of Mersivan). A third expedition from Western Europe, commanded by William IX of Aquitaine and Welf I of Bavaria, also arrived in the Middle East. However, this Aquitanian-Bavarian army was ambushed and massacred by the Seljuks of Arslan, exactly as had happened to those led by William II of Nevers. The survivors of the three expeditions that were organized during 1101 reached Jerusalem a few days before Easter 1102. Some of them went home after completing their pilgrimage, while others were persuaded to remain in the Holy City by Baldwin I. Soon after becoming king, Baldwin had to repulse a Fatimid expedition from Ascalon. The Muslim invading force of 5,000 soldiers was much more numerous than the troops available to Baldwin, who had just 260 knights and 900 infantry. The Crusaders and Fatimids clashed at the Battle of Ramla on 7 September 1101. Initially, the battle went in favourable of the Muslims, who destroyed the Crusaders' vanguard, but Baldwin soon responded with an effective counter-attack conducted with his reserves that broke the Muslim lines and routed the enemy.

During the following years, Baldwin I consolidated his power and became the most prominent ruler of the Crusader states. In 1104, he captured the important port city of Acre, which was followed by Beirut in 1110 and Sidon in 1111. The successes of the King of Jerusalem were made possible by the arrival of new Crusaders and other adventurers from Western Europe, as well as by the decisive support received from the Italian Maritime Republics (Pisa, Genoa and Venice). The Crusaders learned some important lessons from the military events that followed the First Crusade: first of all, that the Seljuks were capable of defeating them on the open field and that they were thus much more dangerous than the Fatimids; and second, that using the land route that crossed Anatolia for supplying their states in the Middle East was very difficult due to Byzantine hostility and the presence of Turks in that region. Recognizing these factors, the role played in the Crusades by the Italian Maritime Republics became increasingly important. Only Pisa, Genoa and Venice had the naval capabilities needed to supply the Christian states in the Middle East, and these cities soon assumed complete control over the new commercial routes that were emerging between Europe and the Levant. Baldwin I proved himself a capable monarch, being

Templar sergeant.
(*Photo and copyright by Ordenskomturei Heppenheim*)

Templar sergeant wearing *chapel de fer* helmet. The latter was popular in the Levant, where temperatures were extremely high. (*Photo and copyright by Ordenskomturei Heppenheim*)

Templar sergeant. (*Photo and copyright by Ordenskomturei Heppenheim*)

Templar standard-bearer. (*Photo and copyright by Ordenskomturei Heppenheim*)

able to defend southern Palestine from several Fatimid invasions coming from Egypt by intercepting them around Ramla. From 1110 onwards, he also had to face frequent Seljuk attacks from the north, which obliged the four Crusader states – the Kingdom of Jerusalem, Principality of Antioch, County of Edessa and County of Tripoli – to combine their military forces. Baldwin knew full well that his realm, like the other western states in the Holy Land, was surrounded by enemy forces and thus tried to improve the existing diplomatic relations with the Byzantine Empire. He also formed a strong military alliance with the only Christian country of the Middle East, the Armenian Kingdom of Cilicia (or Lesser Armenia), by marrying an important Armenian noblewoman named Arda.

In 1113, the King of Jerusalem had to face a massive Seljuk army that was attempting to cross the Jordan River, resulting in a major pitched battle at al-Sannabra. The clash ended in defeat for the Crusaders, but not a decisive one as they were able to avoid complete annihilation. Despite this temporary setback, Baldwin I gradually transformed his realm into a solid feudal state, creating a new warrior nobility in the Holy Land and reinforcing the borders of the Kingdom of Jerusalem. In 1118, however, he died without heirs. The Kingdom of Jerusalem was offered to Eustace III of Boulogne, younger brother of Godfrey of Bouillon and Baldwin I, but the Count of Boulogne was not interested in being given a realm outside Europe and thus refused the offer. The crown was then offered to Baldwin II of Edessa, cousin of Baldwin I, who duly accepted it. After 1118, the Crusader states lived in a state of constant war, coming under increasing military pressure from the Seljuks of northern Syria and Iraq. The Seljuks, having realized that their internal divisions worked in favour of the Crusaders, started to join their military forces against the common enemy. In 1119, the Principality of Antioch came under attack and its army, guided by Roger of Salerno who was ruling in Antioch as regent for Bohemond II, was crushed by the Turks at the Battle of Ager Sanguinis. This was a disaster for the Crusaders, who suffered huge losses, with Roger of Salerno among those killed. Following this setback, Baldwin II was named regent of the Principality of Antioch, but he was later captured during a Muslim raid. The King of Jerusalem spent several years as a captive in Aleppo, but soon after being freed he organized an effective Christian counter-offensive against the Seljuks. Baldwin besieged Aleppo with all his forces, provoking a reaction from the Turks settled in Iraq. The latter assembled a large relief force and marched towards Aleppo. The King of Jerusalem met them at the Battle of Azaz in 1125, and after a long and bloody clash, the Seljuks were defeated and their camp was captured and looted by the Crusaders. Baldwin's victory at Azaz rebalanced the situation after the defeat suffered by the Crusaders in 1119, but hostilities between westerners and Muslims were suspended for only a few years.

In the years following these events, a new and ambitious military leader started to emerge among the Muslims: Zengi, a Turkish aristocrat who was the son of an important warlord who had been the governor of Aleppo. In 1127, Zengi became *atabeg* (ruler) of Mosul and then, in 1128, also of Aleppo. By uniting these two flourishing cities under his rule, he rapidly assumed great political importance. At that time, the Abbasid caliph of Baghdad, al-Mustarshid, was fighting against the Turkish sultan Mahmud II for dominance over Iraq. Zengi supported the former in the ongoing conflict and used the alliance with the Abbasids to his own advantage. In 1130, he tried to conquer the city of Damascus, but he had to content himself with occupying Hama, which had previously been under the control of Damascus' rulers. The years before the ascendancy of Zengi were a period of great political fragmentation for the Middle East, with the Seljuk territories starting to be divided into a series of small states centred on major cities, while the Fatimids were greatly weakened by the defeats suffered at the hands of the Crusaders and the Abbasids struggled for their own survival in Baghdad. After Mahmud II died, Zengi tried unsuccessfully to take Baghdad for himself. In 1135, the ambitious Turkish ruler besieged Damascus for some time, but again without success. Two years later, fearing that Zengi could attack them with a larger army in the near future, the Muslim rulers of Damascus took the unpopular decision to ally themselves with the Christian Kingdom of Jerusalem. From this moment, Zengi became the fiercest enemy of the Crusader states.

In 1127, while Zengi was starting his ascent as a powerful warlord, Baldwin II began thinking about his succession. He had no male heirs but had already designated his daughter, Melisende, to succeed him. The King of Jerusalem wanted to safeguard his daughter's previous inheritance by marrying her to a powerful French aristocrat who could lead the Crusader forces in battle. After examining the characteristics of the various possible candidates, Baldwin chose Fulk, Count of Anjou. A young widower, Fulk was an experienced military commander and a sincere supporter of the Crusades. After receiving Baldwin's proposal regarding the marriage, the Count of Anjou held out for better terms than becoming a mere consort of Melisende: he wanted to be King of Jerusalem, with full powers. Baldwin, having no better alternative, accepted Fulk's request. The French noble then abdicated as Count of Anjou in favour of his son, Geoffrey, and left Europe for Jerusalem, where he married Melisende on 2 June 1129. In 1131, following Baldwin II's death, Fulk and Melisende became joint rulers of the Kingdom of Jerusalem; in practice, however, Fulk acted as sole ruler of the realm. During the previous years, Baldwin II had tried to transform the minor Crusader states into vassals of the Kingdom of Jerusalem. However, when Baldwin died, the other Christian rulers of the Middle East formed an alliance against Fulk in order to weaken the new and inexperienced King of Jerusalem. The first generation of Crusader leaders had finally disappeared with the death of Baldwin II, and new rulers now guided the Christian states: the County of Edessa was governed by Joscelin II, the County of Tripoli was ruled by Pons and the Principality of Antioch was governed by Alice (sister of Melisende). Fulk also had many rivals inside his own realm, since he was resented by the local aristocrats who wanted to have a cousin of Melisende – Hugh II, Count of Jaffa – as their monarch. In 1134, open hostilities broke out between Fulk and Hugh. Allying himself with the Fatimids, Hugh obtained several victories, but he was eventually defeated and exiled from the Kingdom of Jerusalem. During his early years of his rule, Fulk tried to secure the northern borders of his kingdom, for example by arranging the marriage between his loyal supporter Raymond of Poitou and the infant Princess Constance of Antioch. The ascendancy of Zengi, however, represented the most serious menace that the King of Jerusalem had to face. As we have seen, in 1137 Fulk formed an alliance with the governor of Damascus, but the forces of the latter and of Jerusalem were soundly defeated by Zengi, and thus the alliance came to naught. Fulk also stabilized the southern borders of his realm by building several important fortresses, such as Blanchegarde and Ibelin, whose main function was to stop the frequent Fatimid incursions coming from Ascalon. He also erected the famous fortress of Kerak, to the east of the Dead Sea, with the objective of giving the Kingdom of Jerusalem access to the Red Sea.

Fearing that Zengi could soon invade their countries, the three Crusader states of the north allied themselves with the new and warlike Byzantine Emperor John II Comnenus, who entered the Middle East at the head of a large army and joined forces with his new allies, with the objective of moving against Zengi. The Christian army besieged the city of Shaizar, but were soon forced to turn back due to the superiority of the relief forces assembled by Zengi. In 1138, Zengi concluded an alliance with Damascus, apparently renouncing his previous ambition to conquer the city. Nevertheless, the Turkish warlord tried to take the city for himself, but the inhabitants of Damascus asked for help from the Kingdom of Jerusalem. During the following years, Zengi twice besieged Damascus, but without success. Against Fulk's expectations, at least for the moment, he did not attack the Crusader states directly. In 1144, after a short period of relative peace, Zengi finally attacked the Crusader territories of the north with all his military forces. He invested the County of Edessa, the weakest and least westernized of the Crusader states, and after a siege of four months, on 24 December, he captured the city of Edessa. The fall of the County of Edessa was the main reason behind the launching of the Second Crusade. In 1143, both John II Comnenus and Fulk of Jerusalem had died and Zengi seemed to

Templar sergeant armed with falchion. (*Photo and copyright by Ordenskomturei Heppenheim*)

Hospitaller archer. (*Photo and copyright by Ordenskomturei Heppenheim*)

have no real rivals in the Middle East. After having destroyed one of the Crusader states, Zengi became extremely popular among the Muslims of the Holy Land, being praised as the defender of the faith and as a victorious king. The news of the fall of Edessa reached Europe in the early months of 1145, when embassies sent by the Crusader states asked the Pope for military help against Zengi. Pope Eugene III, fearing that the whole Christian presence in the Holy Land could be under threat, issued the *Quantum praedecessores* bull on 1 December 1145, with which he called for a second Crusade to the Holy Land.

The initial response to the new Crusade bull was poor, with none of the major European monarchs seeming to be interested in participating in a military expedition to the Holy Land. The situation changed when Louis VII, King of France, revealed his intention to respond to the Pope's call. Louis had originally planned to organize an independent expedition, one not directed by the Papacy, but he eventually changed his mind and decided to be part of the Second Crusade. The charismatic Abbot Bernard of Clairvaux was commissioned by Eugene III to preach the Crusade, while the Pope also granted to those individuals who participated in the expedition the same indulgences that his predecessor, Urban II, had accorded a few years beforehand for the First Crusade (hence the bull's title *Quantum praedecessores*). A parliament of the major French nobles was convoked at Vezelay in Burgund) in early 1146, with Bernard preaching before the assembly on 31 March. Louis VII, together with his wife, Eleanor of Aquitaine, and the major feudal lords of France, prostrated themselves at the feet of the future saint to receive the Crusaders' insignias. Bernard continued preaching the Crusade in Germany, where reports of his miracles made him extremely popular among the populace. At Speyer, Holy Roman Emperor Conrad III, together with his nephew and future successor, Frederick Redbeard, received the cross from the hands of Bernard. As had happened during the First Crusade, the organization of a new expedition to the Holy Land inspired massacres of Jews in the Rhineland and other areas of Germany. Before returning to his monastery, however, Bernard was able to quieten most of the mobs, meaning the number of victims was much less than during the massacres at the beginning of the First Crusade. While the Crusaders organized themselves in France and Germany, Zengi was assassinated in his court by a slave. Joscelin II, taking advantage of the chaos that followed the death of his enemy, briefly reconquered the County of Edessa and besieged the citadel of the city. However, the successor of Zengi mounted an effective counter-offensive and defeated him decisively in November 1146. The successor of Zengi was his son, Nur ad-Din, who soon demonstrated himself to be a capable military leader.

The German Crusaders decided to reach the Holy Land by travelling overland through the Kingdom of Hungary, regarding the alternative sea route impractical

Templar crossbowman.
(*Photo and copyright by Ordenskomturei Heppenheim*)

because Roger II of Sicily – who had been crowned King of Sicily by the Pope in 1130 after having taken the island from the Muslims – was an enemy of Emperor Conrad. Most of the French Crusaders distrusted the land route through the Balkans since this would have taken them into the Byzantine Empire. Louis did not have a high opinion of the Byzantines and feared that they may attack his troops. After long discussions, however, the French leaders decided to march alongside the Germans in order to better control their movements. From the beginning, the Second Crusade was characterized by the strong political rivalry existing between Louis and Conrad. The German Crusaders – some 20,000 in total – were accompanied by the papal legate and cardinal Theodwin. They passed through Hungary without problems and soon reached Byzantine lands. Here, Emperor Manuel I Komnenos mobilized his troops, fearing that the westerners could pillage his territory. A brief skirmish occurred between some unruly Germans and Byzantine soldiers near Philippopolis, followed by a second clash at Adrianople, but the Crusaders reached Byzantium without having to fight any major clash with the Byzantines. Manuel I Komnenos wished to induce the Germans to cross to Anatolia by the Hellespont in order to keep them away from the Bosporus and from Byzantium. Conrad, however, ignored the advice of Manuel and arrived with his army in front of the Byzantine capital on 10 September. The Byzantine ruler had repaired the walls of his city as a safeguard against any Crusader assault, and the Germans had to encamp outside Byzantium. However, they pillaged the

Levantine archer at the service of the Hospitallers. (*Photo and copyright by Ordenskomturei Heppenheim*)

suburban imperial palace of Philipatium and made depredations in the countryside. Once again, the Crusaders suffered from a lack of food and consequently committed many acts of violence against the local population while searching for supplies. After these events, Emperor Manuel ordered to his troops to face the Crusaders in order to stop their brutal actions. A pitched battle between the Byzantines and the Germans took place just outside the walls of Byzantium. Initially, the Crusaders launched several frontal charges with their heavy cavalry, but these were all repulsed with heavy losses by the Byzantines, who employed large numbers of horse archers. It became apparent that the Germans had no hope of victory despite their courage, with a large portion of their forces – under the command of Conrad – not becoming involved in the battle. The clash ended up as an indecisive victory for Manuel I. Nevertheless, Conrad afterwards crossed into Anatolia with all his men without causing any further damage to Byzantine lands. According to the original plans, the German Crusaders were supposed to wait for the arrival of the French at Byzantium before moving into Anatolia, but the outbreak of hostilities with the Byzantines obliged the Germans to advance on Iconium without waiting for Louis' French forces.

Conrad then took his knights and his best infantrymen to march overland across Anatolia, while the remaining infantrymen and civilian followers – under Otto of Freising – were to advance along the coastal road. On 25 October 1147, at the same location as the First Battle of Dorylaeum, the Seljuk Turks of Rum confronted the Germans on the open field. The Seljuks used their usual battlefield tactics, which were largely unknown to the Germans: they pretended to retreat in front of the enemy advance, before turning back to attack with their fast-moving horse archers the small groups of Crusader knights who had separated themselves from their main army to chase the Turkish skirmishers. Soundly defeated and routed during the Second Battle of Dorylaeum, Conrad and his surviving followers had no choice but to leave Anatolia and fall back to Byzantium. During their retreat, the Germans were harassed on a daily basis by the Seljuks, who attacked the rearguard of the Crusaders and caused many casualties. During one such skirmishes, Conrad himself was seriously wounded. The German Crusaders led by Otto of Freising, who had marched along the Anatolian coast, suffered a similar destiny, running out of food and being ambushed by the Turks near Laodicea on 16 November.

King Louis' French Crusaders included several important nobles: Thierry of Alsace, Renaut I of Bar, Amadeus III of Savoy, William V of Montferrat, William VII of Auvergne and Alphonse of Toulouse. During the crossing of the Kingdom of Hungary and the Byzantine Empire, the French troops caused no incidents. Louis had a largely positive relationship with Emperor Manuel, and thus no serious problems occurred. After some French reinforcements arrived in Byzantium from southern Italy, the

The sword of a Templar knight. (*Photo and copyright by Ordenskomturei Heppenheim*)

Crusaders crossed the Bosporus and entered Anatolia. Despite being under strong pressure from his own court to provide some troops to Louis, Manuel did not actively support the military operations of the French as his own territory had recently come under attack from Roger II of Sicily (who, like his predecessors, wished to invade the southern Balkans). During their march, Louis' Crusaders met the remnants of Conrad's defeated troops at Lopadion. The Germans, still wishing to reach the Holy Land, temporarily put aside their traditional rivalry with the French and joined forces with them. Louis, learning from Conrad's defeat, decided to follow the coastal route instead of marching inland across Anatolia. Emperor Conrad fell sick during the journey and was obliged to return to Byzantium. The Crusaders fought a minor battle with the Seljuks of Rum just outside Ephesus on 24 December before reaching the city of Laodicea. On 6 January 1148, at Mount Cadmos, a larger pitched clash took place between the Crusaders and the Turks. Both sides suffered significant losses and Louis risked being killed, but in the end no decisive victor emerged from the clash. The western knights soon resumed their march, being continually harassed from afar by the Seljuks, who destroyed all the supplies that the French could have taken en route. At this point of the campaign, fearing that his entire army could die of starvation, Louis decided to gather a fleet on the Anatolian coastline at Adalia, and from there to sail for Antioch. After being delayed for a month by storms, only a small portion of the planned ships arrived in the port of Adalia. These few vessels were taken by Louis and the most prominent French nobles, obliging the remaining Crusaders to resume the long inland march to Antioch. Their march, as anticipated by Louis, turned into a disaster, almost the entire Crusader force being destroyed

The personal weapons of a Templar knight. (*Photo and copyright by Ordenskomturei Heppenheim*)

by sickness and raids by the Turks. Louis and his small remaining forces arrived at Antioch on 19 March. Meanwhile, both Conrad and Otto of Freising reached Jerusalem, at the head of very small military contingents.

Baldwin III of Jerusalem, son and successor of Fulk, wanted to employ the newly arrived Crusaders to conquer the city of Damascus, which represented the most serious menace to the survival of the Crusader states. The Muslim governors of the city prepared themselves for a siege, reinforcing their walls and destroying all the water sources located in the surroundings of Damascus. A general council to decide the best target for the newly arrived Crusaders took place on 24 June, during which the decision was taken to attack the city of Damascus. The Second Crusade had been launched to retake Edessa, but now that the new Muslim menace was represented by Nur ad-Din, the Crusader leaders wanted to prevent him from taking Damascus. In total, the Crusaders assembled an army of 50,000 knights and infantry, who marched on Damascus from the west – where the local orchards provided them with a constant food supply. Before they could even complete the building of their encampments, however, they were attacked by the Muslims and forced to abandon their recently occupied positions. Soon after the Crusaders had relocated their camp, they were informed that a large Muslim relief army under the command of Nur ad-

Teutonic knight with mask helmet. (*Photo and copyright by Ordenskomturei Heppenheim*)

Teutonic knight. (*Photo and copyright by Ordenskomturei Heppenheim*)

Din was approaching Damascus. At this point, running the risk of being surrounded by the enemy and of being left without supplies, the leading Crusader nobles refused to carry on with the siege – which had never effectively started – and the army consequently retreated back to the borders of the Kingdom of Jerusalem with Turkish horse archers in hot pursuit. The mutual distrust among the Crusader leaders after the military failure at Damascus led to the inglorious end of the Second Crusade, with neither Conrad nor Louis having any intention of continuing the fight with no hope of victory. In 1154, a few years after the conclusion of the Second Crusade, Damascus was conquered by Nur ad-Din.

Chapter 4

The Third Crusade

The knights and their followers who returned to Europe at the end of the Second Crusade left behind them a weakened Kingdom of Jerusalem, which was seriously menaced by the expansionism of Nur ad-Din. Soon after taking Damascus, he invaded the Principality of Antioch and defeated its forces at the Battle of Inab. During this clash, the ruler of Antioch, Prince Raymond, was killed. Baldwin III of Jerusalem reacted promptly to these events, taking up the regency of the defeated principality and improving his relations with the Byzantine Empire by ceding to it what remained of the County of Edessa. Over time, and especially from 1152, the young Baldwin tried to free himself from the tutelage of his ambitious mother, Melisende. This eventually led to a division of the Kingdom of Jerusalem into two autonomous administrative entities: Baldwin retained the northern part of the realm, while Melisende held the southern section and the Holy City. Just a few weeks after the split of the kingdom, Baldwin invaded the territory of his mother and swiftly defeated her. Following the end of the civil war, in 1154, mother and son were reconciled. However, the conflict had weakened the Kingdom of Jerusalem, while Nur ad-Din had been consolidating his control over most of Syria. Baldwin tried to remain at peace with Nur ad-Din and thus directed his expansionist ambitions towards the southern borders of his realm. During those years, the Fatimid territories were shattered by a series of civil conflicts caused by a succession crisis. In 1153, the Crusaders had successfully besieged and captured the Fatimid stronghold of Ascalon, which stabilized the southern frontier of the Kingdom of Jerusalem. During 1157 and 1158, the warlike Baldwin campaigned in Syria against Nur ad-Din, obtaining some successes despite the internal divisions existing among his most prominent nobles. These victories gave him enough prestige to seek a wife from the Byzantine Emperor, and after complex negotiations with Emperor Manuel, it was decided that he would marry the latter's niece, Theodora. The marriage led to the formation of an alliance between the Byzantine Empire and the Kingdom of Jerusalem, but this was short-lived as Baldwin III died in 1163. He was succeeded by his younger brother, Amalric, who continued the policies of his predecessor.

In 1163, Amalric led an expedition into Egypt, obtaining a clear victory over the weakened Fatimids. However, once the Crusader forces invaded Egyptian lands, the

Detail of the mask helmet worn by a Teutonic knight. (*Photo and copyright by Ordenskomturei Heppenheim*)

Teutonic knight wearing the monastic clothes of his religious order. (*Photo and copyright by Ordenskomturei Heppenheim*)

Fatimids opened the Nile dams and let the river flood to prevent the westerners from advancing any further. In 1164, Amalric invaded Egypt again but soon had to suspend his campaign when Nur ad-Din obtained a great victory over the allied forces of Bohemond III of Antioch and Raymond III of Tripoli at the Battle of Harim, both the Crusader leaders being taken prisoner. In 1167, the Crusaders returned to Egypt and encamped near Cairo. An indecisive battle was fought with the Fatimids, after which Amalric temporarily occupied Alexandria and exacted an enormous tribute from the Muslims. After this Egyptian campaign, Amalric married a Byzantine princess related to Emperor Manuel I and renewed the alliance between the Kingdom of Jerusalem and the Byzantine Empire. The King of Jerusalem then invaded Egypt again and temporarily occupied part of the country. This last defeat was a mortal blow for the Fatimids, who finally lost their hold on power in Cairo. They were replaced by one of Nur ad-Din's leading military commanders, Shirkuh, who became the new ruler of Egypt. In 1169, Shirkuh died and was succeeded by his nephew, Saladin, who became undoubtedly the greatest Muslim military leader during the era of the Crusades, and soon repulsed a Crusader attack against the city of Damietta and launched an invasion of the Kingdom of Jerusalem in 1170. A year later, upon the death of the last Fatimid caliph, Saladin became Sultan of Egypt. In 1174, both Nur ad-Din and Amalric died: Nur ad-Din was succeeded as ruler of Syria by his former vassal, Saladin, while Amalric was succeeded by his leprous son, Baldwin IV. Saladin now controlled the two richest areas of the Muslim world and could simultaneously attack the Kingdom of Jerusalem with large military forces from Syria in the north and from Egypt in the south. In 1177, the first confrontation between Baldwin IV and Saladin took place at the Battle of Montgisard, during which the Muslim forces that were invading the Kingdom of Jerusalem were taken by surprise and completely routed by Baldwin, who, despite his illness, fought with courage.

In 1181, after some years of peace, hostilities between Baldwin and Saladin resumed. The Christian king defeated his opponent again at the Battle of Le Forbelet, but his numerical inferiority was so significant that he was unable to secure a decisive success. While these events took place in the Middle East, in Byzantium an anti-Catholic coup took place inside the imperial court and led to a significant change in the diplomatic policies of the Byzantines, with their alliance with the Kingdom of Jerusalem coming to an end. From 1183, the health of Baldwin IV worsened significantly: he could no longer walk unsupported or use his hands, and he also became blind. Taking advantage of this situation were both Saladin, who prepared his forces for a large-scale invasion of the Crusader states, and Guy of Lusignan. One of the most powerful feudal lords of the Kingdom of Jerusalem, Guy had married

Baldwin's sister, Sibylla. The leprous king had no direct heirs and thus his throne would have been inherited by Sibylla's son, Baldwin. In 1185, Baldwin IV finally died because of his illness, being followed in 1186 by his young nephew, who had been crowned as Baldwin V. Following these events, Guy, who hated all Muslims and was extremely ambitious, was finally crowned King of Jerusalem as the husband of the legitimate heir to the throne (Sibylla). Baldwin IV had spent most of his reign doing two things: limiting the expansionist ambitions of Saladin by fighting effectively against him and trying to conciliate his Christian subjects with the Muslim ones. Guy of Lusignan had completely different ideas: he wanted eradicate the Muslims from the Crusader states of the Levant and thought that defeating Saladin would be quite simple to achieve. In 1183, Saladin had finally completed his conquest of Syria by taking Aleppo, and thus was now ready to wage war on the Kingdom of Jerusalem.

In 1187, hostilities began with a raid launched by Raynald of Chatillon – one of the most prominent Crusader nobles – against a peaceful Muslim caravan. Saladin responded by sending one of his best commanders against the Templars, one of the Military Orders of warrior-monks and the main supporters of Raynald. In the ensuing Battle of Cresson, the Templars were utterly defeated. Saladin then assembled the largest army he had ever commanded (40,000 soldiers, including 12,000 elite cavalry) on the Golan Heights of Syria and invaded the Kingdom of Jerusalem from the north. The great Muslim warlord lured the inexperienced Guy into moving his army of 20,000 Crusaders away from its fortifications and supply bases, by besieging the isolated Christian stronghold of Tiberias. The advancing Crusaders, seeking to free Tiberias from the enemy siege, were constantly harassed by the Muslim horse archers during their march. They soon ran out of water and started to suffer terribly under the summer sun of the Holy Land (the campaign took place in early July). Saladin deployed his army between the Christian forces and the Springs of Hattin, the only source of water that the Crusaders could reach to save themselves. The ensuing Battle of Hattin was the worst defeat ever suffered by the Crusaders in the Levant. Coming under a rain of enemy arrows, the thirsty and demoralized troops were completely surrounded. Most of the foot soldiers deserted, while all the knights were killed or taken prisoner. Guy of Lusignan and Raynald of Chatillon were both captured, together with some other major feudal lords. The Crusaders, having assembled all their forces to fight against Saladin, had deprived most of their fortifications of their garrisons. Taking advantage of this situation, the Muslims easily conquered most of the Kingdom of Jerusalem in less than three months: Acre, Nablus, Jaffa, Toron, Sidon, Beirut and Ascalon all fell to Saladin's men. On 2 October 1187, after a short but dramatic siege, Saladin and his troops conquered the Holy City. Jerusalem had been lost by the Crusaders for the first time in almost ninety years. It was seen as

Teutonic sergeant. (*Photo and copyright by Ordenskomturei Heppenheim*)

a terrible event by the Christians of Europe, and had an enormous psychological impact on them. Now that the Kingdom of Jerusalem had fallen, Saladin seemed unstoppable. It was felt that a new Crusade had to be organized as soon as possible, to save what remained of the Latin states of the Levant (collectively known by the

The personal weapons of a Teutonic knight. (*Photo and copyright by Ordenskomturei Heppenheim*)

French term Outremer). The ruling Pope, Urban III, died soon after having been informed of Jerusalem's fall. He was succeeded by the energetic Gregory VII, who soon called for a new Crusade by promulgating the *Audita tremendi* bull. The three most important monarchs of Western Europe responded to the call: the Holy Roman Emperor, Frederick Redbeard; the King of France, Philip Augustus II; and the King of England, Richard I, the Lionheart.

During recent years, Frederick Redbeard had been the worst enemy of the Papacy in Europe, having conducted several campaigns in Italy with the objective of restoring imperial control over the region. With the decisive help of the Pope, the various Italian cities, jealous of their autonomy, had been able to resist and had even defeated the Holy Roman Emperor on some occasions. This had caused serious damage to the political and military reputation of Frederick, who had to face frequent rebellions by his German princes. At that time, two main political factions were fighting each other in Germany to assume control of the Holy Roman Empire, so Frederick Redbeard needed to restore his authority if he wanted to continue ruling. After Cardinal Henry of Marcy preached the crusade in Germany before a public assembly attended by the Emperor, a diet was held in Mainz on 27 March 1188 and Frederick decided to take the cross together with some of the most important German nobles: Duke Frederick VI of Swabia, Duke Frederick of Bohemia, Duke Leopold V of Austria and Landgrave Louis III of Thuringia. The Holy Roman Emperor planned to assemble his forces at Regensburg on St George's Day and imposed a strict discipline over his men to avoid major massacres of Jews. Emperor Frederick decided to follow the usual land route crossing the Kingdom of Hungary and the Byzantine Empire. He commanded a total of 15,000 men, 4,000 of whom were experienced *milites*. These were joined in Hungary by 2,000 soldiers, led by the younger brother of the local king, who was an ally of Frederick. The crossing of Hungary was completed without major problems, the Germans being supplied with abundant provisions by the locals. Anticipating that the Byzantines would not give his troops a friendly reception, the Holy Roman Emperor divided his forces into four parts before advancing on Byzantium very cautiously. Once at Philippopolis, Emperor Frederick was informed that the Byzantine authorities had no intention to supply him with the provisions he needed provisions, so the Crusaders were obliged to resort to plunder in order to sustain themselves. The Byzantine forces did not engage the Germans in battle as had happened during the Second Crusade, but harassed them by attacking isolated foraging parties. Later, a small Byzantine raiding army of 5,000 soldiers was defeated by Frederick Redbeard. The Crusaders were delayed for six months in Thrace when the Byzantines refused to let them cross the Bosporus, but they finally reached Anatolia. The Seljuk Turks of Rum then assembled an army of 10,000 and attacked the German Crusaders. In the subsequent Battle of Philomelion, which took place on 7 May 1190, the Seljuk horse archers attacked Frederick's camp with a rain of arrows. The Emperor responded by sending 2,000 of his best men out of the camp, who routed the attackers and chased them from the battlefield. After this initial clash, the Turks continued to harass the Crusaders with effective raids, which caused the death of many animals and the destruction of foodstuffs. Being short of supplies, Frederick Redbeard decided to replenish his small reserves by occupying the Rum capital of Iconium. The Seljuks tried to stop the Crusaders and faced them at the Battle of Iconium, which saw the Germans fighting in two groups: the first assaulted the city of Iconium and captured it quite easily, while the second fought on the open field against the Turks. The Emperor fought in the first line with great courage, and his example was fundamental in determining the final victory of his troops. After sacking Iconium, the Crusader army accumulated enough supplies to continue the march. However, disaster then struck for the German army. While crossing the Saleph River on 10 June, Frederick Redbeard's horse slipped and he was thrown against some rocks and drowned. Thereafter, most of the German Crusaders immediately returned to the Holy Roman Empire, anticipating a fresh civil war in view of the upcoming election of a new imperial leader.

Philip Augustus and Richard the Lionheart spent most of the years preceding the Third Crusade fighting against each other as fierce rivals. The Plantagenet Richard owned vast amounts of land in the Kingdom of France and was – at least formally – a vassal of Philip Augustus. The French monarch wanted to transform his realm into the dominant power of Western Europe and thus wished to expel the Plantagenets from France as soon as possible. Richard was a young and warlike monarch, who dreamed of being remembered as his country's greatest king. However, after concluding a truce with Philip Augustus in 1188, King Richard used all his economic resources to raise and equip a large Crusader army. In April 1190, his fleet departed from Dartmouth and sailed to southern France, where the English were joined by the French army. Both Richard and Philip decided that they would reach the Holy Land by sea, in order to avoid the difficult crossing of Anatolia. The monarchs could count on the support of the Italian Maritime Republics, which provided the necessary naval resources to embark their troops. Richard left France from Marseille, while Philip sailed from Genoa in northern Italy. In September 1190, both monarchs arrived in Sicily. The island was the most prosperous region of the Kingdom of Sicily, which was founded in 1130 and comprised most of southern Italy. The realm, as we have seen, was governed by a Norman royal family, meaning its aristocracy had many important connections with the English. In 1189, King William II of Sicily had died and southern Italy had witnessed the beginning of a

The personal weapons of a Teutonic knight. (*Photo and copyright by Ordenskomturei Heppenheim*)

German nasal helmet worn at the time of the First Crusade. (*Photo and copyright by Sericum et ferrum*)

civil war between two pretenders to the throne. On one side was Tancred, cousin of the dead monarch, who seized power in Sicily thanks to the support of his warlike aristocracy; on the other was William II's aunt, Constance, wife of Holy Roman Emperor Henry VI (son of Frederick Redbeard) and legal heir of King William II of Sicily. After siezing power, Tancred imprisoned William II's widow, Queen Joan, who was King Richard's sister, and refused to give her the money she had inherited according to King William's last will. When Richard landed in Sicily, with the port city of Messina becoming the main logistical base of the Crusaders, he demanded the release of his sister and the immediate payment of her inheritance. On 28 September, Tancred duly released Joan but did not pay the sum that Richard had called for. The presence of many English and French soldiers in Sicily added confusion to the political struggles that ravaged the kingdom. The population of the island perceived the strangers as a potential menace and were jealous of the realm's independence. In October, the people of Messina rose up against the Crusaders and demanded that the foreigners leave their land. Richard, in order to show his military superiority to Tancred and Philip, who were both near Messina, attacked the city and captured it on 4 October. After looting and burning Messina, Richard the Lionheart transformed the Sicilian port into his main military base. On 4 March, after several months of increasing tension and thanks to the mediation of Philip, a treaty was signed between Richard and Tancred. According to this, Joan was to receive 20,000 ounces of gold as compensation for her inheritance.

After these events, both Richard and Philip remained in Sicily in order to complete their preparations before sailing to the Holy Land. During this period, however, tensions increased between the monarchs, who were allies on paper only. Frequent skirmishes took place between the English and French soldiers, while Philip Augustus started plotting with Tancred of Sicily against Richard. In the end, however, open hostilities were avoided and both monarchs left southern Italy in the spring of 1191. The Crusader fleet of Richard was dispersed by a storm during the ensuing journey, and some of the king's ships, including those transporting his sister Joan and his promised wife, Berengaria of Navarre, were forced to land in Cyprus. Once on the island, the pair were captured by the local ruler, Isaac Comnenos, a pretender to the Byzantine throne who had transformed Cyprus into his personal realm. In May 1191, Richard arrived in Cyprus at the head of his army, ordering Isaac to release his English prisoners and to give his treasure to the Crusaders. The ruler of Cyprus refused, upon which Richard took the important city of Limassol in retaliation. All the Crusader leaders who were in Cyprus supported the Lionheart, as well as some local magnates who were plotting against Isaac. As a result, by the beginning of July, the King of England was able to conquer the whole island and capture Isaac. The

Norman nasal helmet worn at the time of the First Crusade. (*Photo and copyright by Les Seigneurs d'Orient*)

Display of mask helmets worn during the Second and Third Crusades. (*Photo and copyright by Ordenskomturei Heppenheim*)

occupation of Cyprus was of great strategic importance, since its ports could now act as naval bases for the Crusaders. After assigning his newly conquered territories to the Templars, Richard left Cyprus for Acre on 5 June. Before leaving Limassol, he married Berengaria, the heir of the Spanish Kingdom of Navarre, which bordered with the southern part of Aquitaine (at that time under Plantagenet control) and thus was of great strategic importance for Richard. Cyprus was soon organized as a Crusader state that continued to exist until 1489.

Philip Augustus and his French army reached the Holy Land while Richard the Lionheart was in Cyprus. They soon joined forces with Guy of Lusignan, who had been freed by Saladin, and started besieging the stronghold of Acre. Saladin, knowing the strategic importance of the city, soon assembled a large army and encircled the Christian forces that were besieging Acre. The Crusader troops included a small number of Germans, commanded by Leopold V of Austria, who had not returned to their homeland after the sudden death of Frederick Redbeard. Richard the Lionheart arrived at Acre on 8 June and immediately began supervising the construction of new siege weapons with which to assault the Muslim stronghold. Thanks to his efforts, the city was finally taken on 12 July. At this point, the three main leaders of the Third Crusade – Richard, Philip and Leopold – started quarrelling among themselves over the spoils of victory. The King of England cast down the German standard from Acre, offending Leopold, who soon became an ally of Philip Augustus, who hated the Lionheart with all his heart and had joined the Crusade only in the hope of causing Richard's death or failure. In August 1191, after having been in the Holy Land for just a few weeks, both Philip and Leopold returned to Europe with their armies. Philip intended to attack the Plantagenet territories in France while the Lionheart was away, while Leopold wanted to play an important role in the election of the new Holy Roman Emperor. After the capture of Acre, Richard decided to march on the city of Jaffa, control of which was absolutely necessary for any action against Jerusalem. On 7 September, the forces of the Lionheart and Saladin clashed at the Battle of Arsuf. The King of England commanded 10,000 infantry and 1,200 knights, while the Muslim leader had an army of 25,000 well-trained soldiers (mostly cavalry). Saladin attacked first, but Richard deployed his troops in defensive formation and was able to resist all the enemy assaults. When he sensed the right moment had come, the Lionheart ordered a general counter-attack that determined the outcome of the battle. Saladin was forced to fall back, having lost around 7,000 men. After his victory, King Richard took Jaffa and established his new headquarters there. At this point he tried to negotiate with Saladin in order to end the hostilities, but the peace talks came to nothing. In November 1191, the Crusaders started their advance towards Jerusalem. Meanwhile, the nobles of the

Detail of a great helmet, worn from the Fourth Crusade. (*Photo and copyright by Ordenskomturei Heppenheim*)

Short-sleeved hauberk of chainmail. (*Photo and copyright by Les Seigneurs d'Orient*)

Kingdom of Jerusalem chose to replace Guy of Lusignan as their monarch with the more experienced Conrad of Montferrat. As compensation, the Lionheart sold Cyprus to Guy and his House of Lusignan. During the last weeks of 1191, the Crusaders occupied and refortified Ascalon, which had been razed to the ground by Saladin. Some fierce fighting later took place around Darum on the frontier between the Kingdom of Jerusalem and Egypt, before internal divisions emerged among the Crusaders about how to continue the campaign. Richard was opposed to the idea of investing Jerusalem without the necessary preparations, and wanted to plan an expedition directed against Egypt. Before a decision could be reached, however,

Saladin's army suddenly attacked and captured Jaffa. The Lionheart responded by assembling a token force of 2,000 men, who went to Jaffa by sea and stormed the city. Saladin, counting on his numerical superiority, tried to expel Richard from Jaffa but failed to do so due to the stubborn resistance of the city's defenders. On 2 September, both being exhausted and short of military resources, the King of England and Saladin decided to sign a truce. The Muslim leader promised that he would allow unarmed Christian pilgrims and traders to visit Jerusalem, in exchange for which he was given back the city of Ascalon. Richard the Lionheart departed from the Levant on 9 October 1192: his campaigns had saved the Kingdom of Jerusalem from complete destruction, and thus the Crusader dream – at least for the moment – could continue. On his way home, the King of England was captured by his old rival, Leopold of Austria. Richard was ransomed after two years of captivity but was later killed in France while campaigning against his other old enemy, Philip Augustus. Meanwhile, Saladin, the man who had almost expelled the Crusaders from the Levant, died on 4 March 1193 before the expiry of the truce that he had signed with the Lionheart.

Chapter 5

The Fourth and Fifth Crusades

After Saladin's death, the domains of the great Muslim warlord were contested between his two brothers and three sons. The family members fought against each other for several years, refusing to accept the subdivision of the Syrian and Egyptian lands that had been indicated by Saladin before his death. Henry VI, son of Frederick Redbeard and new Holy Roman Emperor, tried to gain some advantages from these civil wars that shattered the Muslim states of the Middle East. In 1194, he had become the most powerful ruler of the Christian west after assuming control over the Kingdom of Sicily through his marriage to the legitimate heir to the Sicilian throne, Constance of Hauteville. As a result of his increasing personal power, Emperor Henry came into conflict with the Papacy as he could now claim most of the Italian peninsula for himself, thereby surrounding the papal lands. In the hope of improving his relations with the Pope and of consolidating his control over southern Italy, Henry VI organized a new expedition in Germany during 1197 that is commonly known as the German Crusade. The Holy Roman Emperor assembled a substantial army and marched through the Kingdom of Sicily before setting sail for the Holy Land. While still in his Italian realm, however, Henry died of malaria when most of his troops had already left for the Middle East. The German Crusaders landed at Acre and immediately launched an offensive to expel the Muslims from the coastline between Beirut and Tripoli, obtaining some successes such as the occupation of Sidon and Beirut. While marching on Damascus, however, they were informed of Henry VI's death, after which most of them decided to return home without having achieved any spectacular results. By 1200, the internal troubles of the Muslim lands were over, the territories of Syria and Egypt being unified under the rule of the victorious al-Adil, the strongest of Saladin's brothers. As the supreme ruler of the new Ayyubid dynasty that had been created by Saladin, al-Adil renewed the truce that had been signed by his brother with Richard the Lionheart several years before. The Kingdom of Jerusalem no longer represented a strong threat for the Muslims, its territory having been reduced to a few coastal settlements and not comprising the Holy City. Before the expiration of the new truce on 1 March 1204, al-Adil started to change his attitude towards the Crusader states, since in the previous years he had

Detail of a mitten made of chainmail. (*Photo and copyright by Sericum et ferrum*)

Crusader kite shield. (*Photo and copyright by Les Seigneurs d'Orient*)

been able to complete the unification of the Muslim lands and could now turn his attention towards the small Christian domains.

Pope Innocent III, fearing that the Ayyubids would now destroy the Christian presence in the Holy Land, called for a new Crusade. Nevertheless, his requests for the organization of a new military expedition were ignored by most of the European monarchs, and also by the Maritime Republics of Pisa and Genoa that were currently locked in conflict. Innocent III planned an invasion of Egypt, understanding that was where the Ayyubids' centre of power lay. He sponsored the forming of a contract between the few Crusaders who responded to his call (mostly from France) and the Maritime Republic of Venice, which would provide the necessary vessels to transport the Christian troops to Egypt in exchange for the payment of a large sum of money. The Venetians supported the new Crusade with just one objective in mind: weakening as much as possible the Byzantine Empire in order to gain dominance over the commercial routes crossing the Adriatic Sea. At that time, the Byzantines were experiencing serious internal troubles, the throne of Emperor Isaac II Angelos having been usurped by his brother, Alexios III Angelos, through a military coup. The legitimate ruler had been blinded, but was still alive and in search of allies who could help him seek revenge. After gathering in Venice, the Crusader army – consisting of 4,000 knights and 8,000 infantrymen – was asked to pay the agreed sum of 85,000 silver marks to the Venetians. The problem was that the Venetians had assembled a much larger fleet than was now needed, the Pope having originally requested vessels capable of transporting over 30,000 soldiers. Since there were only 12,000 Crusaders now gathered in Venice, they did not have enough money to pay for all the ships that had been provided by the Venetians. In order to assemble the requested Crusader fleet, the Venetians had halted their commercial activities and had employed 20,000 of their men to crew these vessels. As a result, if they were not now paid, they would have experienced serious financial problems.

Ultimately, the Crusaders paid just a portion of the sum that had previously been agreed and the Venetians proposed to the Crusader leaders that they pay their debts by fighting for Venice against the port of Zara in Dalmatia. The Catholic coastal city had previously been dominated by Venice, but in 1181 it had rebelled against the Italian Maritime Republic and had formed a strong alliance with the Kingdom of Hungary. The Hungarians wanted to transform Zara into a strong rival to Venice in the Adriatic Sea, battling for dominance over local naval routes. The Crusaders agreed to attack Zara in return for the Venetians then transporting them to the Holy Land. On 24 November 1202, the city of Zara was taken after a brief siege by the Venetians and the Crusaders, who pillaged it and demolished its fortifications. Innocent III excommunicated the Crusaders for their actions, but by that time control of the expedition was in the hands of the Venetians. While wintering in Zara, the Crusaders received an offer from the son of the deposed Byzantine Emperor, Isaac II Angelos, who proposed to pay their entire debt owed to the Venetians, give them 200,000 silver marks and place the Orthodox Church under Papal authority in exchange for the Crusaders promising to depose the usurper who ruled over Byzantium. The proposal was swiftly accepted by the Venetians and later also by most of the Crusader leaders. Consequently, on 23 June 1203, the Crusader fleet arrived at Byzantium and started preparations to besiege the city. The Byzantine defenders tried unsuccessfully to oppose the landings; the Venetians forced their passage in the Bosporus, and thus the proper siege began. On 17 July, employing several impressive siege machines and attacking also from the sea, the Crusaders launched their assault on Byzantium. The attackers were initially repulsed, but it was just a question of time before they could enter the city. Consequently, some leading Byzantine officers abandoned their ruler and chose Alexios IV, son of Isaac II Angelos, as their new emperor. It soon became apparent that the new Byzantine Emperor was unable to pay the promised sum of money to those who had supported him. In addition, the Byzantine population had no intention of acknowledging a ruler who had been placed on the throne by foreigners. As a result of this situation, Alexios IV was soon deposed by his subjects and hostilities recommenced between the Byzantines and the Crusaders. The siege of Byzantium was resumed, the city finally falling on 12 April 1204. The Byzantine capital was set on fire and sacked for three days, in an orgy of violence that led to the destruction of many ancient works of art. The true Crusader spirit died during those crucial hours. Following the fall of Byzantium and the inglorious end of the Fourth Crusade, the Balkan territories of the Byzantine Empire were partitioned between the Venetians and the Crusader leaders: the island of Crete and some coastal areas were given to Venice, while the former Byzantine mainland became known as the Latin Empire. The latter was partitioned between the French Crusaders and was organized as four minor states: the Kingdom of Thessalonica, Principality of Achaea, Duchy of Athens and Duchy of the Archipelago. Meanwhile, Byzantine refugees founded their own rump states in Anatolia and Epirus – the Empire of Nicaea, Empire of Trebizond and Despotate of Epirus – with the aim of reconquering the southern Balkans in the future.

Despite the failure of the Fourth Crusade to even reach the Holy Land, Innocent III did not renounce the idea of organizing a new expedition aimed at restoring the Christian presence in the Kingdom of Jerusalem. Times, however, were changing quite rapidly, and the most powerful European monarchs were no longer interested in risking their armies to reconquer some strips of coastal land in the Levant. In reality, what remained of the Crusader states was not menaced by al-Adil, who was much less warlike than his more famous brother Saladin. From 1201–02, an exceptionally low Nile River had caused the complete failure of the Egyptian crops, which led to the spreading of famine and pestilence in the Muslim lands. The Ayyubids, at least for the moment, were not interested in a new war against the Crusaders, being more worried by the possibility that the powerful Maritime Republics could attack Egypt from the sea. For these reasons, al-Adil continued to renew the truce with the Christians and did not plan any major military campaign. Yet if the European monarchs were no longer interested in launching a new Crusade, the same could not be said of their subjects, as religious zeal was still particularly strong among commoners. In 1212, a shepherd boy from the Rhineland named Nicholas started preaching a new Crusade and – thanks to his personal charisma – gathered several thousand peasants who were determined to follow him to the Holy Land. Most of Nicholas' followers were children or young boys, with no experience of life. They

Crusader kite shield, bearing decorative symbols related to the Kingdom of Jerusalem. (*Photo and copyright by Les Seigneurs d'Orient*)

had been fascinated by the Crusader ideals but had no knowledge of what they were going to face. In the end, only a few of them ever reached the Holy Land, where they became dispersed. Also during 1212, a French shepherd boy named Stephen, from Cloyes, assembled a multitude of 30,000 commoners for a new expedition to the Holy Land. Like those guided by Nicholas, Stephen's children and boy 'Crusaders' mostly died of starvation even before embarking for the Holy Land, and the few of them who survived were killed or enslaved by bandits as soon as they reached the Middle East. The events that took place during 1212 in Germany and France, collectively known as the Children's Crusade, impressed Innocent III, revealing that popular support for the crusading expeditions was still very strong. The Pope, however, died in 1216 before the new Crusade he had planned could be launched.

As we have seen, French knights had always made up the bulk of the Crusader military forces. At that time, however, the Kingdom of France was shattered by the

Crusader sword. (*Photo and copyright by Les Seigneurs d'Orient*)

bloody internal conflict known as the Albigensian Crusade. This was organized by the Papacy and the King of France to eradicate the Albigensian Heresy from southern France. In reality, however, the Crusade was nothing other than a military campaign launched by the King of France against his vassals of southern France, who resented the central power of the monarchy. The Holy Roman Empire was also experiencing a period of internal conflict, with two pretenders to the throne fighting against each other, while the Kingdom of England was shattered by the conflict that saw King John – known as Lackland – fighting against the most prominent barons of his realm. As a result of this situation, the new Pope, Honorius III, had no choice but to look outside Western Europe to find some Christian leaders who would be interested in the new Crusade. It was Andrew II, King of Hungary, who eventually responded to the Papacy's call and assembled his forces in the summer of 1217. The King of Hungary, accompanied by a significant number of German Crusaders under Leopold VI of Austria, departed from Zagreb and was transported to the Holy Land by the Venetian fleet. On 9 October 1217, the Crusaders landed on Cyprus, from where they soon moved to Acre. Arriving in the latter city, the Crusader leaders started to plan the first moves of their campaign. Having very little knowledge of the Middle East, they marched towards Damascus and crossed the Jordan River after having obtained some minor successes over the Muslims. However, they soon realized that the forces of al-Adil that they were facing were extremely numerous, so they returned to Acre without having achieved anything. The Crusaders next moved against the Ayyubid stronghold of Mount Tabor, but after a short siege the whole operation failed and, having suffered significant casualties, they once again returned to Acre. Andrew II and his Hungarians, no longer interested in the Crusade – which they had only started to have the support of the Pope and in the hope of gaining some former Byzantine lands – left the Middle East in February 1218 after having achieved practically nothing.

The Fifth Crusade, however, continued, the French and German Crusaders who had been mobilized during the previous months still determined to fight against the Muslims. Their leader was John of Brienne, a warlike aristocrat who had a solid military reputation. John, following the will of the Pope, wanted to attack Egypt as it was the Ayyubids' centre of power. He planned to attack the important port city of Damietta, where the Egyptian naval resources were concentrated. Damietta was not far from Alexandria and could be easily attacked from the sea. Counting on the decisive support of the Italian Maritime Republics, John of Brienne was sure that the occupation of the city could have caused serious trouble for the aging al-Adil. On 27 May 1218, the first Crusader ships arrived at the harbour of Damietta, located on the right bank of the Nile. The Ayyubids soon responded by moving some of their troops from Syria to Egypt and massing an army a few miles south of Damietta. The city had impressive fortifications, which consisted of three walls of varying heights as well as of dozens of towers. In front of the city, on a small island of the Nile, there was the Chain Tower, a massive fortification whose name derived from the impressive iron chains – blocking the entrance to Damietta's inner harbour – that stretched through it. The only way to invest Damietta from the sea was to seize the Chain Tower, which was garrisoned by hundreds of chosen soldiers. The Crusaders' siege of Damietta began on 23 June with an assault on the Chain Tower. The attackers employed two special ships during the assault: one consisted of two vessels bound together, with scaling ladders mounted on their decks, while the other had a small fortress built on its mast, from which stones and javelins could be thrown. This first attack was

The Fourth and Fifth Crusades 103

Crusader sword. (*Photo and copyright by Ordenskomturei Heppenheim*)

Crusader falchion. (*Photo and copyright by Ordenskomturei Heppenheim*)

repulsed quite easily by the Muslims, after which the Crusaders built another special ship that combined the best features of the previous two, with a revolving ladder that extended far beyond the ship. On 24 August, through effective use of the new special vessel and after hours of bitter fighting, the Crusaders were finally able to take the Chain Tower and cut the defensive chains of Damietta's inner harbour. A few days later, al-Adil died, causing great difficulties for the Muslims. The son of al-Adil, al-Kamil, became the new sultan and had to reorganize they city's defences. He blocked the course of the Nile by scuttling several ships a mile upstream from Damietta and recruited more soldiers. The winter of 1218–19 passed without any major actions, the conditions of the Nile being unsuited to combat.

Before the campaign could resume, the energetic papal legate, Pelagius Galvani, reached the Crusaders. Pelagius wanted to conquer Damietta as soon as possible, since he considered Alexandria the real target of the expedition. During the following months, the Crusaders repulsed several Ayyubid attacks against their camp. They also built a floating fortress on the Nile to improve their defences, but this was soon captured by the Muslims after having been seriously damaged in a violent storm. The storm also flooded the Crusader camp, badly damaging their supplies. After new Crusader reinforcements arrived at Damietta, al-Kamil decided to open negotiations in order to avoid further losses. He offered to surrender most of the Kingdom of Jerusalem to the Crusaders, together with a truce of several years, in exchange for their promise to evacuate Egypt. Such a generous offer was the result of al-Kamil suffering internal difficulties, the sultan being under constant threat from his rivals to the throne. Pelagius refused the offer, despite the fact that many of the Crusaders were dying from illness. The Egyptian climate and the humid environment of the Nile proved unsustainable in the long run for the Europeans, so many Crusader leaders, including Leopold VI of Austria, decided to return home. On 8 July 1219, in a bid to save the situation with the troops still under his command, Pelagius launched multiple attacks on Damietta. These were mostly conducted by soldiers and sailors from the Maritime Republics, but all were repelled by the defenders. On 29 August, Pelagius organized an attack on al-Kamil's camp, but this was also a complete failure. After these events, the Muslims again tried to make peace, offering to return the portion of the True Cross that had been lost by the Crusaders at the Battle of Hattin as well as the release of all Christian prisoners. Nevertheless, Pelagius refused this offer too. In September 1219, Francis of Assisi, founder of the Franciscan Order of friars, arrived in Egypt and – after visiting the Crusader camp – crossed over the lines to preach to and attempt to convert al-Kamil. Hoping that Francis was a peace emissary sent by the enemy, al-Kamil received him with courtesy. The Ayyubid sultan did not convert after hearing Francis preach, but expressed his admiration for

Crusader knife. (*Photo and copyright by Les Seigneurs d'Orient*)

the Italian friar (who was canonized in 1228). Francis remained in Egypt for some time and then went to Acre, where he established the Province of the Holy Land, a priory of the Franciscan Order whose members obtained the privilege of acting as the guardians of the holy places in the Middle East (something that they continue to do to this day). The long siege of Damietta continued for several more months, until the defenders ran out of supplies and al-Kamil decided to evacuate the city. The Muslim forces established their new main base downriver at Mansurah, waiting for the next move of the Christian forces. At this point of the campaign, John of

Different points of Crusader spears. (*Photo and copyright by Ordenskomturei Heppenheim*)

Brienne left the Crusader camp with several of his followers, leaving Damietta under Pelagius' direct control. The early months of 1220 saw no major fighting taking place, the Crusaders being too weak to mount an effective offensive, while the Ayyubids employed all their resources to fortify Mansurah. In early July 1221 the Crusaders advanced south, having as their main objective the conquest of Cairo. The whole

Crusader mace. (*Photo and copyright by Ordenskomturei Heppenheim*)

operation was poorly planned and badly conducted by Pelagius, who did not bring enough food supplies with his advancing army. The Muslims had the great advantage of knowing the terrain over which the Crusaders were moving, especially the many canals that characterized this portion of Egypt. The Ayyubid sultan sent a fleet of agile warships down the Nile, north of the advancing European knights, the Muslim soldiers disembarking to block the Crusaders' line of supply and communication with Damietta. Pelagius tried to return to his starting positions, but soon learned that his troops had been completely surrounded. Sultan al-Kamil then had the sluices along the right bank of the Nile opened to flood the area where the Crusaders were

Display of Crusader maces. (*Photo and copyright by Ordenskomturei Heppenheim*)

stationed. His men being in no condition to fight, Pelagius sued for peace on 28 August. The papal legate offered to withdraw from Damietta in exchange for the freedom of his men and the return of the relic of the True Cross. The Muslims accepted these terms, and subsequently all the remaining Christian troops were evacuated from Egypt, bringing the Fifth Crusade to an inglorious end.

Chapter 6

The Sixth, Seventh and Eighth Crusades

After a long power struggle, Frederick II, son of Henry VI, finally became Holy Roman Emperor while the Fifth Crusade was still taking place. The young monarch, who was also King of Sicily, needed the support of the Papacy to consolidate his power in Germany and thus promised that he would participate in the ongoing Egyptian expedition with a large army. In the end, however, Frederick II did not participate in any active way to the final stages of the Fifth Crusade, realizing that the venture no longer had any chance of success. In 1225, the new Pope, Gregory IX, started to apply pressure on the Holy Roman Emperor to oblige him to take the cross and take advantage of the difficult political situation in the Muslim lands. At that time, al-Kamil was fighting some of his relatives for dominance over Ayyubid territory. On 25 July 1225, Frederick II, who was then the most powerful monarch in Western Europe, promised the Pope that he would depart on a new Crusade by 15 August 1227, the agreement to be respected under the pain of excommunication. During the following months, the Holy Roman Emperor also became King of Jerusalem, marrying the heir to the throne of the Holy City, Isabella II. However, as Frederick II could not count on the support of all the major aristocrats of the Kingdom of Jerusalem, he issued a decree under which the German Teutonic Order was given the same privileges as the Templars and Hospitallers. This move, however, was not enough to secure him the loyalty of all the nobles of the Crusader states, many of whom still considered John of Brienne (father of Isabella II) to be their legitimate monarch. In May 1227, al-Kamil, concerned about the stability of his sultanate, sent peace proposals to the Holy Roman Emperor before he could leave southern Italy with his troops. These attempts to find a compromise, however, came to nothing since Frederick was now obliged to guide an expedition to the Middle East or he would be excommunicated. The Holy Roman Emperor was somewhat torn, however, as he had spent most of his childhood in Sicily and was a lover of Muslim culture, spoke Arabic, admired Islamic culture and had many Muslim intellectuals inside his cosmopolitan court. Nevertheless, by early September 1227, the first contingents of German Crusaders had reached the Holy Land, forcing the Muslims out of Sidon and installing the Teutonic Knights in Montfort Castle, which was located north-east of Acre. The outbreak of a plague, however, slowed down the transportation of more troops to the Middle East. Pope Gregory IX, thinking that the plague was just an excuse used by Frederick II to not launch an effective expedition, excommunicated the Holy Roman Emperor on 29 September. Following these events, Frederick began secret negotiations with the Muslims. After the plague ended, the Emperor finally sailed to the Middle East with the bulk of his forces and – after a short period spent on Cyprus – arrived in Acre on 7 September 1228. Once in the Holy Land, Frederick understood that it would be impossible for him to organize any military operation: his troops were too few and most of the Crusader nobles living in the Middle East did not respect his authority due to his excommunication by the Pope. Furthermore, once in Acre, he was informed that papal military forces were preparing an invasion of the Kingdom of Sicily during his absence. At this point, the Emperor decided to negotiate peace terms with al-Kamil in order to leave the Holy Land as soon as possible and with a diplomatic success. On 18 February 1229, a peace treaty was signed, according to which a large portion of the territories that made up the Kingdom of Jerusalem before the Battle of Hattin were returned to the Crusaders, including the Holy City of Jerusalem, Bethlehem, Nazareth, Sidon,

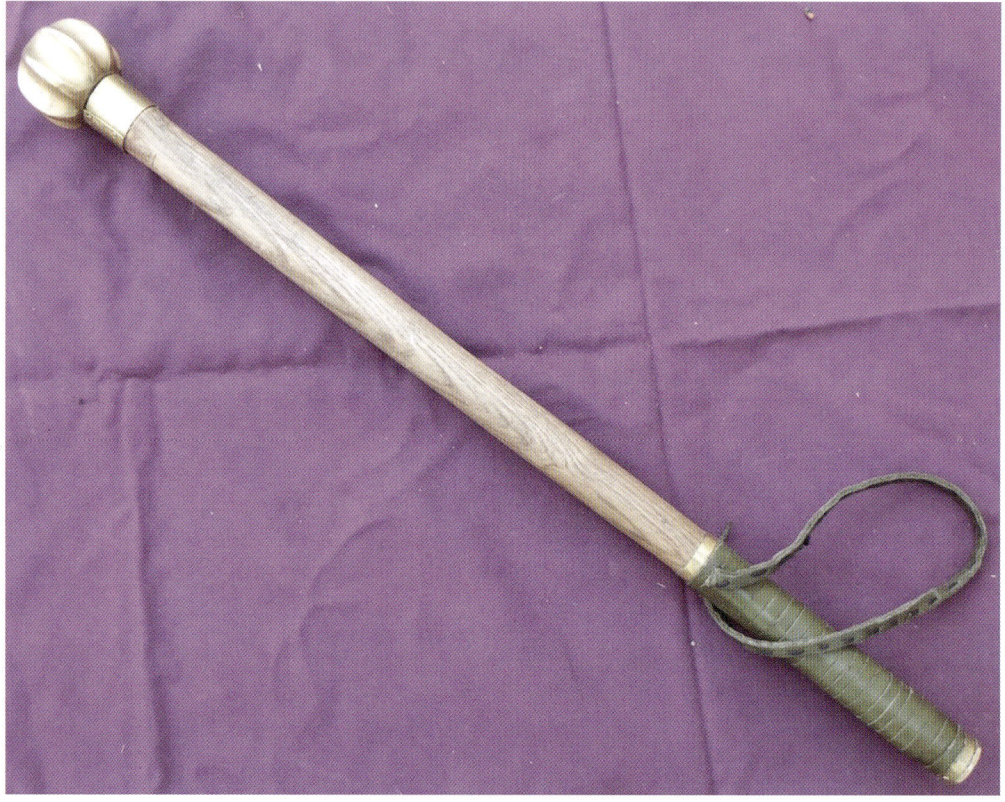

Crusader mace. (*Photo and copyright by Ordenskomturei Heppenheim*)

Crusader axe. (*Photo and copyright by Les Seigneurs d'Orient*)

Jaffa and Toron. Most of the Palestinian coastline was also returned to the Crusader states. In Jerusalem, however, the Muslims kept possession of the Temple Mount, al-Aqsa Mosque and the Dome of the Rock. The signing of the Treaty of Jaffa marked the end of the Sixth Crusade and was a great personal success for Frederick II, who had been able to retake Jerusalem without fighting a single battle. It should be noted, however, that both the rulers of the Crusader states and the Pope were extremely unhappy about the outcome of the Sixth Crusade because it had not led to the defeat of the weakened Ayyubids.

In late 1238, before the truce of ten years stipulated by the Treaty of Jaffa ended, the Papacy started to send emissaries across Europe to preach for a new expedition to the Holy Land. Several major nobles responded to the call, in particular the King of Navarre, Theobald I, who left Europe from Marseilles at the head of 1,500 knights in August 1239 and reached Acre on 1 September the following month. After joining forces with the knights of the Crusader states, Theobald I's troops conducted some minor skirmishes against the Muslims. On 12 November, a group of around 500 knights split off from the main Crusader army to conduct a raid near Gaza. However, the small force was intercepted by a large contingent of Egyptian troops. The ensuing Battle of Gaza was a disaster for the Crusaders, with most of the 500 knights who had left the main army being massacred. Thereafter, the Muslims attacked Jerusalem and seized it on 7 December after a month-long siege. The so-called Barons' Crusade of Theobald I seemed at this point to be condemned to failure, but a civil war then broke out between the Muslim ruler of Damascus and that of Egypt. The Europeans took advantage of the situation by stipulating a treaty with the Emir of Damascus, according to which most of the Holy Land was returned to the Crusaders. The expedition thus ended, without having seen much fighting, in early 1241. The Barons' Crusade returned the Kingdom of Jerusalem to its largest size since 1187, but this new positive situation for the Crusader states was not to last for long. In 1244, the Ayyubids of Egypt allied themselves with the Khwarazmians – former vassals of the Seljuk Turks who had been expelled from their home territories in Central Asia by the arrival of the Mongols – and attacked the Kingdom of Jerusalem with a large army. The Holy City was reconquered again by the Muslims after a brief siege and most of its buildings were destroyed. In October 1244, at the Battle of La Forbie, the forces of the Kingdom of Jerusalem were routed by the Muslims: 5,000 Crusaders were killed and another 800 were taken prisoner.

After these events, which threatened to end Western Europe's presence in the Middle East forever, the Papacy called for yet another Crusade. The only major European monarch to respond was Louis IX of France, who was moved by his deep religious beliefs. Louis was a capable monarch and a true Christian believer: he spent most of his life fighting for the freedom of the Holy Land and was proclaimed a saint soon after his death (earning the nickname of the Crusader King). The Seventh Crusade began in 1248, after three years of preparations. Louis IX collected large sums of money from across his realm and was able to assemble a substantial military force, consisting of 3,000 knights and 12,000 foot soldiers. The army sailed first to Cyprus, where the King of France negotiated with the leaders of the Crusader states before deciding to attack Egypt. According to Louis' plans, by conquering Egypt, the Crusaders would acquire a base from which to attack Palestine from the south as well as a source of grain supplies that would resolve their logistical problems. In 1249, the French Crusaders landed at Damietta on the Nile and took it – quite easily – on 6 June, the Egyptians putting up largely feeble resistance. After spending the winter in Damietta, King Louis decided to move southwards and march on Cairo. The advancing Crusader vanguard, however, was intercepted by the Muslims at Mansurah and soundly defeated. The Egyptians then mounted a major attack against the main enemy army, which obtained some success. The stubborn Louis, despite being in a difficult situation, decided not to withdraw to Damietta and instead besieged the Egyptian positions at Mansurah. The besieging operations proved fatal for the Crusaders, who were in no condition to operate away from Damietta for a long period of time. Most of them died of illness or starvation, determining the final failure of the Seventh Crusade. In March 1250, Louis fell back on Damietta, but what remained of his army was intercepted by the Egyptians at the Battle of Fariskur. Most of the Crusaders were killed and those few who survived were forced to surrender since they were completely surrounded by the enemy. Louis was captured and fell ill with dysentery. He was ransomed after two months of captivity, in exchange for the payment of a large sum of money. Damietta was reoccupied by the Muslims, and thus the Seventh Crusade also ended in failure.

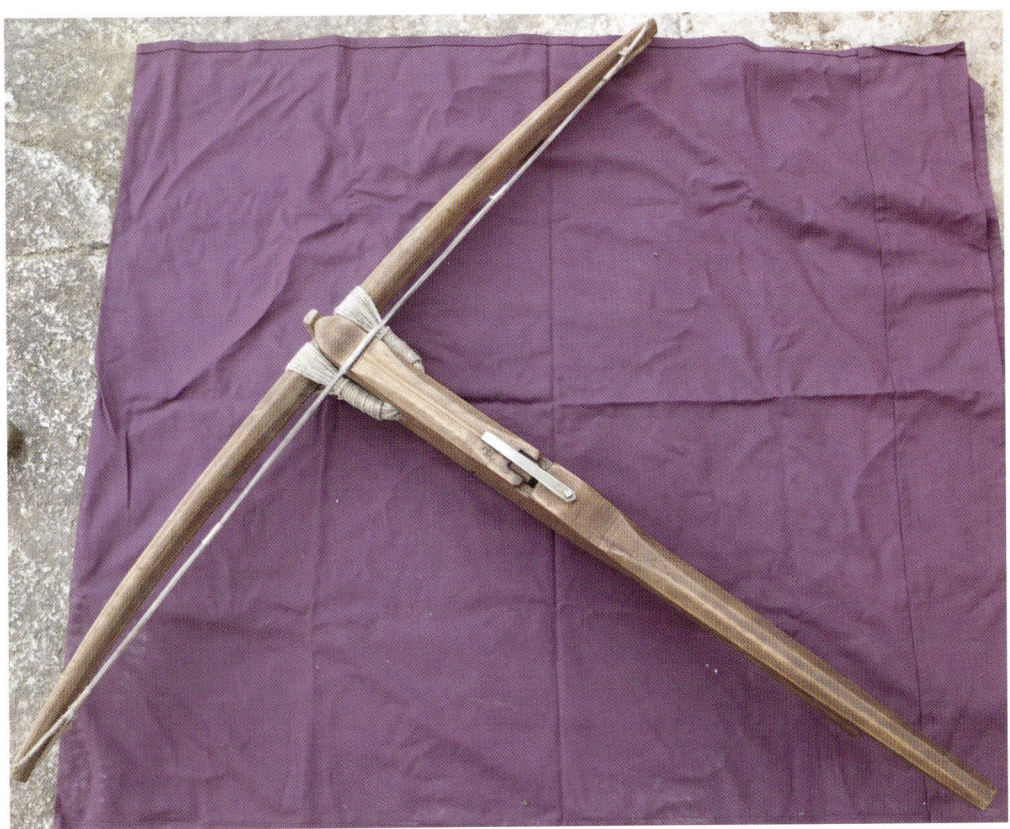

Crusader crossbow. (*Photo and copyright by Les Seigneurs d'Orient*)

Despite having been unable to conquer Egypt, Louis of France did not lose interest in crusading: he established a permanent French military garrison in Acre and continued to send financial aid to the Crusader states during the period from 1254–65. In 1266, his younger brother, Charles of Anjou, defeated Manfred of Swabia (an illegitimate son of Holy Roman Emperor Frederick II) and conquered the Kingdom of Naples for himself. Meanwhile, the political situation in the Middle East changed completely within a few years, with the Mamluks, professional soldiers of Turkish origin who had served for almost a century in the Ayyubid armies of Syria and Egypt, revolting against their employers and creating their own autonomous dynasty under the guidance of the ambitious Baibars. The latter became the new Sultan of Egypt and soon came to control most of Syria thanks to his great military abilities. Differently from their Ayyubid predecessors, the Mamluks were not interested in co-existing with the Crusader states in the Middle East and were motivated by a renewed religious zeal. From 1265, Baibars started to launch large-scale attacks on the Crusader states in a bid to wip them from the map of the Mediterranean world. The Mamluks' strategy regarding the Crusader fortresses located along the coast of the Levant was not to capture and reutilize them, but to destroy them so that they could not be used in the future by fresh waves of Crusaders from Europe. Between 1265 and 1268, the Christian Kingdom of Cilician Armenia, the only regional ally of

Saracen heavy cavalryman. (*Photo and copyright by Les Seigneurs d'Orient*)

Seljuk heavy cavalryman. (*Photo and copyright by Les Seigneurs d'Orient*)

the Crusader states, was devastated by the Mamluk troops and the following fortified Crusader cities were lost: Arsuf, Halba, Arqa, Safad, Ramla, Jaffa and Antioch. The Crusader states were no longer able to deploy substantial armies in the field, having not received any significant help from Europe for many years. In the early summer of 1270, King Louis of France organized a new Crusade, with the aim of distracting Mamluk military resources from Baibars' offensive against the remnants of the Crusader states. Initially, it was planned to land the French troops in Acre, but Charles of Anjou convinced his brother to attack the Muslim city of Tunis instead. Tunis was ruled by an autonomous caliph and was not part of Mamluk territory, so the expedition had no hope of damaging Baibars from the beginning. Charles of Anjou wanted to annex Tunis to his Kingdom of Naples, which was the main reason behind the decision to divert Crusader forces from the Middle East to Tunisia. The French landed on the Tunisian coast on 18 July 1270 and met no strong Muslim resistance. They built a large fortified camp and prepared to advance inland, but an epidemic of dysentery then swept through their ranks. King Louis tried to besiege Tunis, but he too fell sick and died just before the arrival of Charles of Anjou. On 30 October, the siege of Tunis was lifted and a peace treaty was signed between the Crusaders and the local Muslims. The French troops returned to Europe and the Eighth Crusade ended without any major fighting having taken place.

Prince Edward, son of Henry III of England, joined the Eighth Crusade too late to play any significant role, only arriving with his troops in Tunis when the French had already made peace with the Muslims. Prince Edward, however, was determined to win some military glory by fighting against the Muslims; as a result, at the end of April 1271, the English Crusaders – who had in the meantime gone to Sicily – voyaged to Acre to carry out what became known as the Ninth Crusade or Lord Edward's Crusade. However, this is today considered by most historians as a simple appendix of the Eighth Crusade. Following Louis of France's death, Baibars decided to attack the County of Tripoli in order to destroy it, as he had already done with the Principality of Antioch. The Mamluks besieged the fortified city of Tripoli with a large army, but they had to abandon the complex siege when Edward and his English Crusaders arrived at Acre. Edward's men were too few to confront the Mamluks on the open field, only being able to launch a handful of raids from Acre, which accomplished little more than burning some Muslim villages and crops. In December 1271, Edward repulsed a Mamluk attack on Acre, but he was in no condition to mount an effective counter-offensive. During recent years, the Mongols, coming from their heartland in Central Asia, had conquered Iran and Iraq. They had tried to conquer the Middle East in 1260, but had been soundly defeated by the Mamluks. Edward then tried to form an anti-Baibars alliance with

The Sixth, Seventh and Eighth Crusades 117

Seljuk heavy cavalryman armed with axe.
(*Photo and copyright by Les Seigneurs d'Orient*)

Seljuk heavy cavalryman armed with spear.
(*Photo and copyright by Les Seigneurs d'Orient*)

The Sixth, Seventh and Eighth Crusades 119

Seljuk heavy cavalryman armed with scimitar.
(*Photo and copyright by Les Seigneurs d'Orient*)

the Mongols, but his plans came to nothing because they were no longer interested in conquering the Middle East. Having no further hope of securing victory, the prince negotiated a ten-year truce with Baibars, according to which the Mamluks were to halt their attacks against what remained of the Crusader states. Edward returned to England in 1274, following the death of his father, to be crowned king as Edward I. Some years later, in 1289, the Mamluks gathered a large army and invested what remained of the County of Tripoli. The capital of the Crusader state was besieged and taken after a bloody assault. Two years later, the Mamluks besieged Acre, the last Crusader stronghold in the Middle East and the final remnant of the Kingdom of Jerusalem. Acre had been the doorway to the Holy Land for many years and had thus been heavily fortified by the Crusaders, with inner and outer walls reinforced by a total of twelve towers. The Mamluks invested the Christian stronghold with a force comprising experienced soldiers, but had to face the fanatical resistance of the defenders. The attackers pushed forward barricades and wicker screens for several days in order to reach the fosse located before the outer defences of the city, then began mining and bombarding the walls. The defenders responded by launching several attacks against the enemy camp, which achieved some success. After peace talks failed, the Mamluks spent many weeks preparing their final assault on Acre, mining several of the city's towers and building more siege machines. On 18 May 1291, the Mamluks attacked along the entire length of the city's walls, overcoming the defenders and pouring through the breaches that they had produced during the previous weeks. The Crusaders, in particular the Templars and Hospitallers, fought with enormous courage to defend their positions but – after a stubborn resistance – most of them were slaughtered. Only a few defenders survived and managed to leave Acre by sea before the end of the day's dramatic events. The Templar fortress located at the western tip of the city resisted for another ten days, but in the end it too was occupied by the Mamluks. With the fall of Acre, the long history of the Crusaders finally came to an end.

Chapter 7

Crusader Armies

The various Crusader armies existing between 1096 and 1291 belonged to two main categories: the multinational military forces assembled in Europe and sent to fight in the Middle East, and those locally raised in the Crusader states that were created after the success of the First Crusade. Both categories had the usual feudal military organization, but the contingents of the Crusader states had some distinctive peculiarities. For example, they usually comprised variable numbers of locally raised soldiers from the Middle East (known as Turcopoles) as well as troops provided by the few regional allies of the Crusaders (Cilician Armenia and Georgia, two Christian realms of the Middle East). The armies of the Crusader states also included the elite forces of the Military Orders.

Feudal contingents: organization and equipment

When the Crusades began, the dominant social and military model of Western Europe was the feudal system, under which each ruling monarch parcelled the lands of his realm out to the nobles who were loyal to him. As a result, thousands of knights were enfeoffed – i.e. they were given a fiefdom by their king. The lands of Western Europe were not given only to lay aristocrats, but also to clerical nobles (Princes of the Church). Each noble, whether lay or clerical, was required to provide knights who were under his orders to the king in case of war. Over time, the military system based on sub-infeudation – the division of the aristocrats' major fiefdoms into minor ones given to knights – became increasingly complex. For example, when the number of knights sub-infeudated within his fiefdom fell short of that owed to the monarch, a single feudal tenant could maintain sufficient harness to equip some knights making up his personal household in order to make up the difference. Most of the nobles had personal households consisting of loyal knights who provided military service in exchange for money rather than land. These retinues of professional soldiers could consist of just a few individuals but also of larger contingents, depending on the wealth of the aristocrat paying them. The compulsory military service based on the feudal military structure – known as *servitium debitum* – could last for a maximum of sixty days (later reduced to forty) after mobilization. Initially, the mobilized feudal knights could also be sent to fight abroad, but from the beginning of the thirteenth century most of the European *milites* refused to serve outside their homeland. Some major nobles were granted what was known as a money fief, whereby they were not required to send their knights to the king in case of war but had to provide a fixed sum of money with which the monarch could recruit mercenary soldiers. This system, however, never became particularly popular during the period of the Crusades. Feudal military mobilization usually caused malcontent among the aristocrats of a realm, who preferred to pursue their own personal interests rather than those of the monarchy. As a result, after 1150, there were some attempts by the feudal monarchies to introduce a new form of partial mobilization that was based on a quota system. According to this model, the king summoned only a portion – usually one third – of those knights owing feudal military service and called upon those remaining at home to support the mobilized *milites* economically through the *scutage* system. This was based on a simple principle: if exempted from military duties, each vassal was to pay a certain sum of money that was to be used for buying/maintaining the personal military equipment of those vassals who had been mobilized. By the middle of the thirteenth century, however, this system of partial mobilization was no longer in use since it had failed to achieve its objective.

The knights holding a fiefdom, however, were not the only professional soldiers who could be called to serve by a feudal monarch. There were also tenants of an inferior social status who were known as sergeants. These, despite not being nobles, had been given a land property by the monarchy in exchange for their military service. Originally, the sergeants were required to serve as heavy infantrymen, since they did not have the economic resources to maintain a horse, but many of them eventually became rich enough to equip themselves exactly like the noble *milites*. Cavalry was not the only component of the feudal armies, as there were also sizeable contingents of infantry. According to the existing military organization, each able-bodied free man aged between 16 and 60 and living in any fiefdom of the realm could be called to serve by his overlord in case of war. Those who refused military service were subject to fines or to the loss of their property. Such service was usually only of short duration and had practically no costs for the royal authorities, since the members of this general levy were expected to provide their own arms and provisions and were not paid by the monarch for their military service. Each knight could mobilize a certain number of peasants who lived and worked on his land in order to form a small retinue of poorly equipped infantrymen. In case of large-scale foreign invasions, it was the king's responsibility to call up for the general levy of all the able-bodied men of his realm. Most European freemen were peasants, who spent their lives working in the fields and following the natural cycles. As a result, on most occasions, service

Seljuk heavy infantryman. (*Photo and copyright by Les Seigneurs d'Orient*)

Saracen heavy infantryman. (*Photo and copyright by Les Seigneurs d'Orient*)

Seljuk heavy infantryman. (*Photo and copyright by Les Seigneurs d'Orient*)

in the general levy could last only for very limited periods – sixty days, later reduced to forty – and the king had to pay his freemen if any additional period of service was needed. On most occasions, only one freeman from each five units of land was required to join the general levy when it was mobilized for a campaign. The selected individual was expected to be equipped with a spear and shield, to have provisions for two months and to receive a wage, all provided by the other men living on the five units of land from which he was levied. The sergeants/minor landowners were frequently employed by knights as the commanders of their feudal infantry retinues. It should be noted, however, that the smallest contingents of peasant foot soldiers could be commanded by parish priests, while the largest ones were usually under the orders of local royal officials. The Assize of Arms of 1181, a document implemented by Henry II of England detailing the kind of personal equipment that every knight and feudal infantryman had to carry in war, divided the commoners into three military categories according to their economic capabilities: those possessing at least sixteen marks of chattels or rents (such as the richest sergeants) were to equip themselves as knights with full panoply; those with at least ten marks of chattels or rents (for example the poorest sergeants) were to equip themselves as heavy infantrymen with helmet, hauberk of chainmail and spear; and those possessing less than ten marks of chattels or rents were to equip themselves with helmet, quilted gambeson jacket and spear. Shields, being defensive weapons, were not mentioned in the document, but were carried by all soldiers. Curiously, Henry II also promulgated an Assize of Arms for his French territorial domains in 1181, but this prescribed different panoplies for the foot troops belonging to the second and third categories. The soldiers of the second category were to have helmet, hauberk of chainmail, spear and sword; while those of the third category were to have helmet, quilted gambeson, spear and sword or bow and arrows. These differences are interesting because they show two things: that most of the English commoners were too poor compared with their French counterparts to own a sword, and that the bow was not yet a popular alternative to the standard infantry spear.

The feudal contingents of the Crusader states were quite similar to those raised in European countries, but they did have some peculiarities. Firstly, the peasants living on the lands of the Crusader states were not Christians like their overlords, and thus were not willing to serve in the armies of those who had invaded their lands. Consequently, no contingents of feudal infantrymen could be levied in the Crusader states from the local commoners. Sometimes, feudal levies were obtained from the few Christians (Armenian or Syrian) living on the lands of the Crusader states, but these were mostly employed only to perform auxiliary duties like building encampments or fortifications. In addition to the above, the new countries created by the Crusaders in the Levant were always quite small, which meant that their territory could not be divided into many fiefdoms and that the number of knights living permanently in Outremer was never particularly high. The Kingdom of Jerusalem, for example, comprised just four major fiefdoms – Jaffa, Galilee, Tansjordan and Sidon – and another twelve minor fiefdoms. The lack of land was compensated for by the large-scale employment of the money fief, which never became particularly popular in

Saracen heavy infantrymen. (*Photo and copyright by Les Seigneurs d'Orient*)

Saracen standard-bearer. (*Photo and copyright by Les Seigneurs d'Orient*)

Fatimid heavy infantryman. (*Photo and copyright by Les Seigneurs d'Orient*)

Europe. At the time of its maximum territorial extent, the Kingdom of Jerusalem could field a total of 650–700 knights, half of these having standard fiefs and living in the countryside, while the other half had money fiefs and lived in the major cities of the realm (Jerusalem, Nablus and Acre). The Principality of Antioch could field some 400 *milites*, the majority of whom owned money fiefs, whereas the County of Edessa and the County of Antioch could muster only around 100 knights each. All the *milites* of the Crusader states were paid for their horse and personal equipment when serving outside the borders of their state. They also enjoyed a form of insurance called restor, according to which if a knight lost his horse in battle his monarch was to replace the animal at his own expense. The Catholic Church obtained large land properties in the Holy Land after the success of the First Crusade. Although these ecclesiastical properties did not provide *milites* to the lay governments of the Crusader states, there were significant numbers of sergeants who – depending on their personal wealth – could serve on foot or mounted. By the time of the Battle of Hattin in 1187, the Kingdom of Jerusalem could deploy a total of 5,000 sergeants, around half of which were provided by the Patriarch of Jerusalem and the various bishops of the Catholic Church established in the Holy Land. The Principality of Antioch had around 3,000 sergeants, while the Principality of Edessa and Principality of Tripoli had some 700 each. Differently from what happened in Europe, military service by the knights and the sergeants had no precise time limits in the Crusader states. After the disaster of Hattin, the nature of the Crusader states' military forces changed in a significant way, with feudal knights starting to be replaced by mercenary *milites* and sergeants replaced by urban militias raised in the major cities. These cities, being isolated and almost constantly under siege, improved their military structures during the course of the thirteenth century. The urban militias, however, could be employed only for static defensive duties and never left the walls of their cities.

By the outbreak of the First Crusade, the general appearance of the European heavy knights had not changed from that of the Normans who had followed William the Conqueror at the Battle of Hastings in 1066. The *milites* were still protected by a hauberk or shirt of mail, which was made of several thousand interlocking metal rings. The dimensions of each hauberk could vary considerably, with the sleeves either only to the elbow or covering the full arm. The bottom of the hauberk generally reached the knees, but could be longer or shorter. Producing this armour was a long and costly process, which only nobles could sustain; nevertheless, the use of chainmail among knights was practically universal. By the middle of the twelfth century, the personal protection of a knight also included other elements made with mail, including *chausses* (armour protecting the legs) and gloves. At that time, separate coifs of mail for protection of the head were not yet in use, and the portion of chainmail protecting

Fatimid light infantryman. (*Photo and copyright by Les Seigneurs d'Orient*)

Fatimid light infantryman. (*Photo and copyright by Les Seigneurs d'Orient*)

Fatimid heavy infantryman. (*Photo and copyright by Les Seigneurs d'Orient*)

head and neck was simply part of the hauberk. The standard conical helmet with nasal of the Normans was still very popular, but a semi-spherical version of it with full facial mask was increasingly common to find. During the last decades of the twelfth century, due to the increasing diffusion of the crossbow on European battlefields, most of the knights started to abandon their previous helmets with no protection for the face (except for the nasal) and replaced them with new ones that had different patterns of facial masks. The latter were fixed and initially gave protection only to the front part of the face, but they gradually started to have larger dimensions in order to also cover the sides of the face. As a result of this process, the helmets gradually transformed into great helms providing complete protection to the head. Regarding shields, there was a progressive transition from the Norman kite shield to the new triangular shield that was used for most of the Middle Ages. The main offensive weapons of the knights were the spear and the long sword. The chainmail was worn over a padded garment known as a gambeson, which offered additional protection to its wearer. The adoption of closed helmets made it impossible to recognize the identity of the knight on the field of battle. To solve this problem, heraldry saw a rapid growth, with each noble family starting to develop a distinctive emblem. This was initially painted only on the shield of each knight, but it was later also reproduced on a new piece of garment that came into use: the surcoat. The latter was worn over the hauberk and initially had no embroidered decorations. Over the following decades, the heraldic display of each knight was completed by a coloured crest that was placed on top of the helmet. Until 1200, war horses were not protected with any specific piece of equipment. However, during the early thirteenth century, the widespread adoption of the crossbow led to the creation of new defensive elements specifically designed for horses. Initially, these protected only the head, but were later improved in order to protect the entire body of the horse. They could be made from quilted material or chainmail.

The second half of the thirteenth century saw a decisive development of plate armour, which started to be worn in combination with the traditional hauberks. This process of evolution was encouraged by the increasing diffusion and effectiveness of the crossbow. Initially, plate armour was mostly made of *cuir bouilli* (boiled leather) and consisted of disks protecting the shoulders and knees. Soon, however, leather started to be substituted by metal, and new pieces of plate armour – such as greaves – came into use. The protection of the head and neck, meanwhile, had been improved thanks to the introduction of a hood made of chainmail – known as a *camail* – that was separated from the hauberk. The torso of the *milites* started to be protected by a robust coat of plate armour, formed by many small and flat pieces of iron that were riveted together inside a thick fabric garment (buckled at the back). During this period, most of the knights began using maces or axes as an alternative secondary

Seljuk officer. (*Photo and copyright by Les Seigneurs d'Orient*)

Seljuk light cavalryman. (*Photo and copyright by Les Seigneurs d'Orient*)

Crusader Armies 137

Seljuk horse archer.
(*Photo and copyright by Les Seigneurs d'Orient*)

weapon to the long sword. By the end of the thirteenth century, the hauberk of each knight was usually supplemented by a series of additional defensive elements of plate armour, which could be richly decorated: *vambraces*, *cuisses*, gauntlets, *poleyns* and *sabatons*. Meanwhile, a new form of open helmet, known as the *chapel de fer*, had become popular among the *milites*. This wide-brimmed helmet was initially designed for the infantry, but since it was much more comfortable to wear than the various models of great helm, the *chapel de fer* was also adopted by knights. Sergeants were equipped more or less like the knights, but their armour was usually lighter than that of the *milites*. After the knights adopted plate armour, for example, most of the sergeants continued to wear simple hauberks.

The poorest feudal infantrymen had no military equipment to speak of: they went to war with their ordinary clothes and were mostly armed with their agricultural tools. The luckiest of them had a padded gambeson and a simple helmet (usually of conical shape, later replaced by the wide-brimmed *chapel de fer*). The foot sergeants were much better equipped than the peasant levies. They all had helmets and frequently wore a full chainmail over their gambeson. Some of them even had *chausses*, while many were armed with long pikes that had to be used with both hands. The quilted gambeson – the armour of the poor – was quite popular among the archers and crossbowmen too. It was usually made of linen or wool, with the stuffing being obtained from different materials such as scrap cloth or horse hair. Quilted hoods for protection of the head were usually worn together with the gambeson. The latter, during the thirteenth century, was improved with the addition of some new components like quilted collars or quilted gloves. The archers usually carried a sword and a knife in addition to the bow; sometimes they could also have a small round shield, but they wore no armour or only had a light gambeson. Crossbowmen often had hauberks or gambesons, worn together with a *chapel de fer*. Since their main weapon had to be used with both hands, they had no shields and thus were usually deployed behind a line of *pavisiers* – specialized infantrymen equipped with a large and flat shield known as a *pavise*. These, however, became popular in Western Europe only after the end of the Crusades.

Native contingents: organization and equipment

The armies of the Crusader states comprised varying numbers of professional soldiers, distinct from the foot or mounted sergeants, who were recruited from the local Muslim communities. These were known as Turcopoles, a term that literally meant 'sons of the Turks' and was introduced by the Byzantines to indicate the Seljuk mercenaries serving in their regular military forces. The Turcopoles were natives of mixed parentage (in most cases having a Muslim mother and a Christian father) or Muslims who had converted to Christianity. A direct product of the Crusades, they were the heirs of a peculiar military tradition. They could fight on foot or mounted, depending on their personal wealth, exactly like the Crusader sergeants, and were professional soldiers and thus were regularly paid for their military service. Most of them were equipped as light cavalry and fought in the traditional Seljuk way, with composite bows. The Kingdom of Jerusalem, by the time of the Battle of Hattin, could deploy around 4,000 Turcopoles. They were commanded by an independent officer (known as a Turcopolier) who was specifically charged with their administration. Most of the Turcopoles were under the service of the Templars and Hospitallers, who employed them as lightly armed and fast-moving skirmishers or scouts. The Turcopoles rode indigenous horses and used the same personal equipment as their opponents, which comprised composite bow and light spear. The spears were frequently replaced by throwing javelins. A sword and a mace were carried by most of the Turcopoles for hand-to-hand fighting. For protection, quilted gambesons or short-sleeved hauberks were worn, together with simple conical helmets. Sometimes, lamellar cuirasses of the same type used by the Muslims were employed. The Turcopoles rode on light Turkish saddles. After the fall of Acre in 1291, the few surviving Turcopoles, still loyal to their overlords, went to the island of Cyprus.

The forces of the Crusader states, especially those of the County of Tripoli, also comprised significant numbers of Maronite Christians from Lebanon, mountain warfare specialists who served as excellent foot archers. After the fall of the County of Tripoli, a large number of Maronite warriors went to Cyprus together with their families and continued to fight for the Crusader cause. The Armenians of Cilicia were particularly numerous in the County of Edessa and the Principality of Antioch, where they made up a considerable portion of the local population. They served both as light infantrymen and heavy cavalry, acting as auxiliaries during some of the most important campaigns. The independent Kingdom of Cilician Armenia, which continued to exist as an autonomous entity until 1375, was the most loyal ally of the Crusader states. It usually provided some 1,000 cavalrymen and 2,000 infantrymen to the Crusaders when needed. The Christian Kingdom of Georgia, albeit being quite far from the Holy Land, was the only other regional ally of the Crusader states in the Middle East. Its soldiers, equipped as light infantry or heavy cavalry like the Armenians, were of excellent quality and made a significant contribution to the Christian cause during the later Crusades. The military role played by the Armenians and the Georgians in the period from 1096–1291 is very little known, largely because the Crusaders never had a high opinion of their local allies since they were not Catholic Christians. It should be noted, however, that the Armenian

Fatimid foot archer.
(*Photo and copyright by Les Seigneurs d'Orient*)

Seljuk cavalry helmet. (*Photo and copyright by Les Seigneurs d'Orient*)

Fatimid infantry helmet. (*Photo and copyright by Les Seigneurs d'Orient*)

and Georgian states, by fighting with the same methods employed by their Muslim enemies, resisted much longer than the Crusader states. The arrival of the Mongols in the Caucasus and the emergence of the Mamluks in the Middle East led to the fall of Christian Armenia and Georgia several decades after Acre was conquered by the Muslims. Together with Cyprus, Armenia and Georgia were the last bastions of Christendom in the Levant.

Crusader Armies

Military Orders: organization and equipment

Following the events of the First Crusade, fighting for the Christian faith became part of the chivalric code respected by all the feudal knights of Western Europe. In consequence, the two great ideologies of medieval Europe – chivalry and faith – came together as one in the new Crusader states of the Holy Land. The practical result of this fusion was the creation of the so-called Military Orders, ecclesiastical orders that had a double nature: religious and military. The creation of the Military Orders, which were made up of "warrior-monks" who chose to devote their entire lives to the pursuit of the noble Crusader ideal, was achieved by finding a compromise between the original pacifist nature of the Christian faith and the new warlike religious ideals introduced in Western Europe with the beginning of the First Crusade. After Jerusalem fell to the Crusaders in 1099, the Europeans who settled in the Holy Land had to face the problem of how to protect the new pilgrim routes that were now in the process of being opened across the Middle East. The scarce military forces

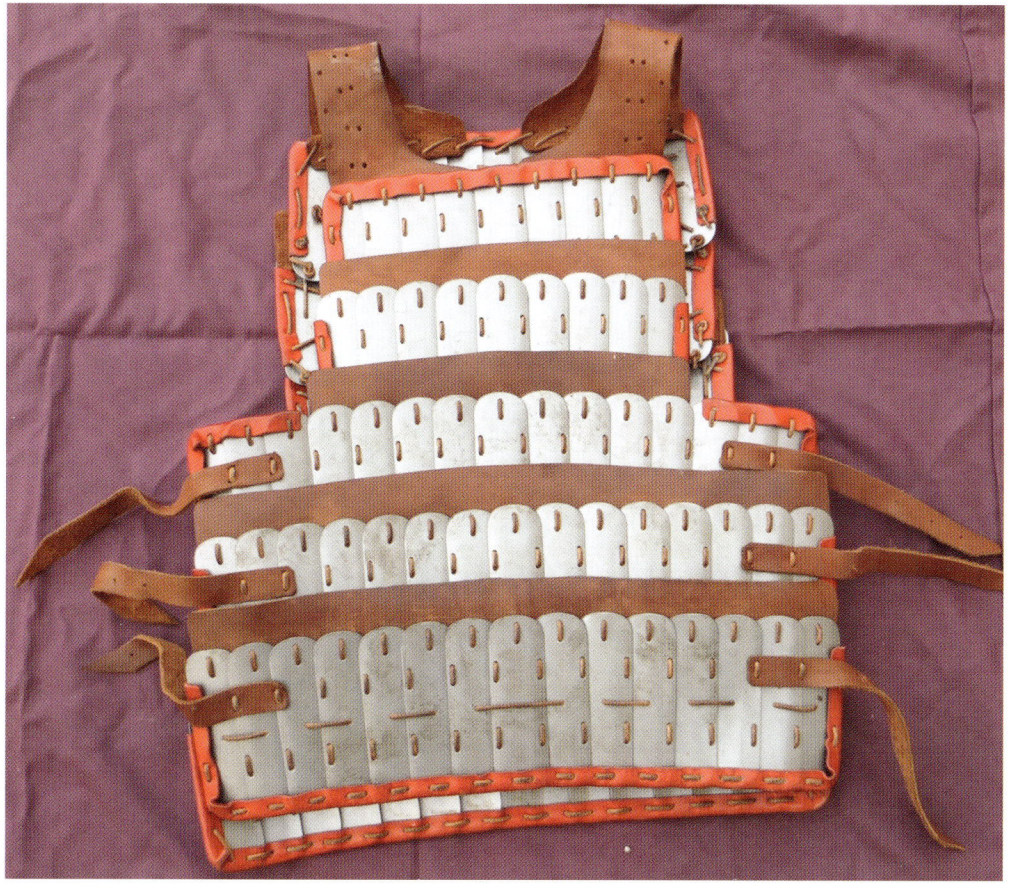

Seljuk corselet. (*Photo and copyright by Les Seigneurs d'Orient*)

Saracen corselet. (*Photo and copyright by Les Seigneurs d'Orient*)

available to the new Crusader states could not be scattered across the many holy places to act as their garrisons, so a new category of troops – specifically charged with protecting the convoys of pilgrims and with garrisoning the most important strongholds of the Crusaders states – had to be formed. Initially, small groups of Crusader knights voluntarily took on the task of performing these important roles, but it soon became apparent that more effective permanent military corps needed to be created. Travelling in the Holy Land after the First Crusade could be extremely dangerous for European civilians, as the Muslims controlled most of the countryside and frequently launched incursions against the Christian convoys. Pilgrims could be ambushed by the numerous bands of brigands that were active in rural areas

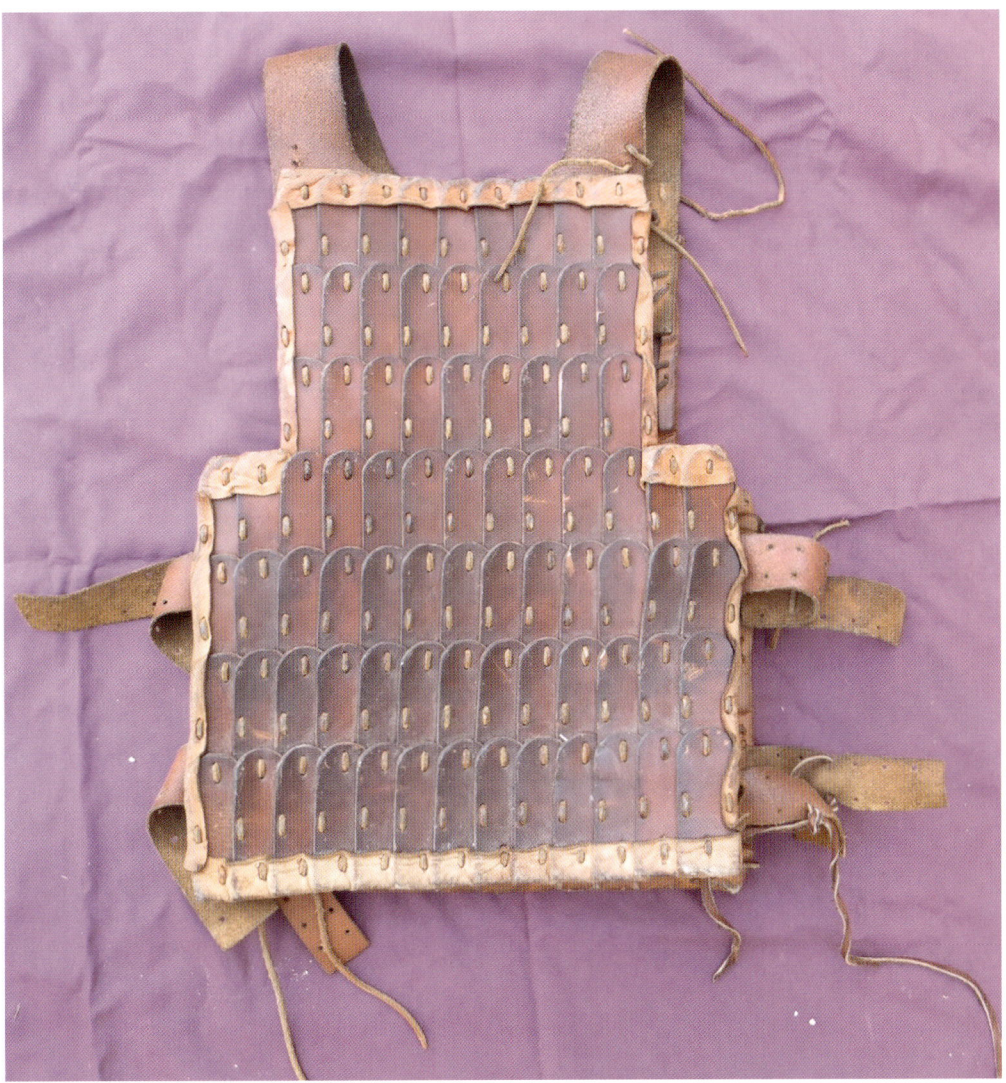

Saracen corselet. (*Photo and copyright by Les Seigneurs d'Orient*)

between the major cities or could be hampered by the lack of food and water supplies. (They did not know where the few wells were located, for example, and needed local guides in order to survive.) Soon after their foundation, the Military Orders became without doubt the most important source of professional troops for the armies of the Crusader states, due to their permanent nature. It should be noted, however, that their ecclesiastical nature meant the Military Orders responded only to the Pope, and that they could act independently from the Kingdom of Jerusalem, for example by concluding treaties and alliances without asking permission from any lay political authority. The Military Orders eventually started to have a network of fortresses across the Holy Land, as the defence of all the major strongholds of the Kingdom of Jerusalem was entrusted to them. The warrior-monks transformed their fortresses into major military bases, which were used to protect the convoys of pilgrims and to slow down Muslim invasions, but also became important commercial centres since they started to have substantial economic interests in the Levant. In addition to their territorial possessions in the Middle East, the Military Orders were given estates from large numbers of benefactors throughout Western Europe, and it was from these rich estates that they obtained the human and economic resources needed to continue operating in the Holy Land. Several Military Orders were created during the Crusades, but only three of these rose to prominence and became effective powers: the Hospitallers, Templars and Teutonic Knights.

Hospitallers: Around 1070, a group of merchants from the Italian Maritime Republic of Amalfi founded the Hospice of Saint John the Almoner near the Church of the Holy Sepulchre in Jerusalem. The hospice was a place of rest for the Christian pilgrims who went to the Holy City, where they could be given food and recover after a long and perilous journey. Transporting pilgrims by sea to the Holy Land was a fundamental part of the business of the Italian merchants from Amalfi, so it was natural for them to establish such a hospice in Jerusalem. During the siege of Jerusalem that took place during the First Crusade, the Hospice of Saint John was temporarily closed by the Fatimids, but it was soon reorganized as a hospital to care for the sick after the Crusaders' victory. The hospital was administered by a number of Benedectine monks coming from Amalfi, who soon received substantial economic support from the first rulers of the Kingdom of Jerusalem. By 1120, after also having been given some land properties by the lay government, the monks had been able to create a chain of hospices and hospitals across the Holy Land, and thus were becoming increasingly important. In 1113, the monks of the Hospital of Saint John were granted papal protection with the promulgation of a special bull, and were formally organized as a new ecclesiastical order: the Order of the Hospital of Saint John. Initially, the Hospitallers only provided assistance to the pilgrims coming from Europe, establishing their own bases in the major ports of the Levant. Over time, however, they also started to perform some military duties. Around 1126, for example, they were tasked with providing armed guards for the protection of the Holy Sepulchre; in later times, the Hospitallers also became known as the Knights of the Holy Sepulchre. From 1136, the Order was given some important strongholds by the lay rulers of the Crusader states and started to have sizeable military forces at its disposal for garrisoning these fortresses. Initially, the Hospitallers simply hired mercenary knights to perform military duties, but a number of them soon became

Crusader Armies 147

true warrior-monks. By 1168, the Hospitallers could field 500 knights, most of whom were still mercenaries or *milites* who had been given some land belonging to the Order in exchange for their military service. After the Battle of Hattin, the military component of the Hospitallers became larger and increasingly important.

By the end of the twelfth century, they had assumed their definitive internal organization, whereby membership of the Order could be of three different kinds. The first group was the brother priests, who fulfilled the original duties of the Hospitallers by running the hospices and hospitals for pilgrims. There were also the brother knights and the brother sergeants, both of whom performed military duties. The basic organizational unit was the commandery, which consisted of twelve members who were placed under an officer known as the commander. The various commanderies were grouped into larger units known as provinces or priories, each of which was commanded by a prior. The priories were assembled into larger units known as grand commanderies, and by the end of the Crusader period these had been grouped

Seljuk padded jacket. (*Photo and copyright by Les Seigneurs d'Orient*)

Seljuk round shield. (*Photo and copyright by Les Seigneurs d'Orient*)

into seven *langues*, or tongues, consisting of grand commanderies whose members all spoke the same language and came from the same geographical area: Provence (southern France), Auvergne (central France), France (northern France), Aragon (Iberian peninsula), Italy, England and Germany. As is clear from this subdivision, the initial Italian predominance inside the Order had soon vanished after the First Crusade, being replaced by a French one. The Hospitallers were guided by a Grand Commander of the Order, who was supported by the following superior officers: the Marshal, who was the commander of the military forces; the Hospitaller, who was in charge of the non-combatant brother priests; the Treasurer, who administered the economic resources of the Order; the Drapier, who acted as the quartermaster of the military forces; and the Turcopolier, who commanded the Turcopoles who were at

Seljuk round shield. (*Photo and copyright by Les Seigneurs d'Orient*)

the service of the Hospitallers. The knights and the sergeants of the Order of Saint John – and those of the other Military Orders – were equipped exactly like their lay equivalents. Every *miles* was allowed to own four horses and to have two squires, while each sergeant could have two horses but no squires. The squires were employed in combat only in case of emergencies, and were under the command of an officer known as a Gonfanonier. By the beginning of the thirteenth century, a strong rivalry had developed between the Hospitallers and the Templars, which sometimes caused violent confrontations between members of the two Military Orders. At the peak of its power, the Order of Saint John could deploy around 600 brother knights and 900 brother sergeants, in addition to several hundred auxiliary Turcopoles and mercenary knights/sergeants (the latter being mostly employed to perform garrison duties in the

Order's many fortresses). Until 1259, the heraldry of the Hospitallers consisted of a white cross placed on a black background; thereafter it was modified according to the Pope's will and started to consist of a white cross on a red background.

Templars: The Templars were created in northern France in 1115 by two knights named Hugue de Payens and Godfrey de Saint Adhemar. The pair recruited seven other *milites* in order to form a small voluntary association that had as its main objective that of escorting pilgrims on their way from Jerusalem to Jericho, and thence to the site of Jesus' baptism in the Jordan River. In 1118, the nine knights swore an oath before the Patriarch of Jerusalem to defend the pilgrims and observe the monastic vows of poverty, obedience and chastity. The beginnings of the Templars were extremely humble: Hugue de Payens and Godfrey de Saint Adhemar, for example, had only one horse between them at the beginning of their activities in the Holy Land. The first official denomination of the Templars was the Poor Knights of Christ. From the beginning, the new religious organization had a distinct military nature, differently from what happened with the Hospitallers. The Poor Knights of Christ were subsidized by the Patriarch of Jerusalem and were thus at the latter's orders, but Baldwin I was particularly impressed by their devotion and decided to give them quarters in a wing of his royal palace. As a result, the future Templars started to act as an unofficial police force inside the royal palace of Jerusalem. Their new quarters were located on the supposed site of the Temple of Solomon, and it was for this reason that they started to be known as the Knights of the Temple or the Knights Templar. The number of knights wishing to become Templars rose quite rapidly, and over time it was felt that they should be organized permanently along monastic lines, with special rules allowing them to live as monks but also to perform as warriors. In 1124, Hugue de Payens returned to Europe to ask for guidance in the formulation of such new rules, and visited the Council of the Catholic Church that was taking place at Troyes in France. The Council officially gave the Templars the statutes that formally established them as a military/religious organization. The statutes of the Templars – greatly influenced by those of the Cistercians – were elaborated by Bernard of Clairvaux, a great protagonist of the Second Crusade.

The daily life of the Templars was characterized by harsh discipline and unqualified obedience. All the members of the Order were dressed the same, lived together very soberly and did not have any private property. Futile occupations and immoderate laughter were forbidden, together with all other vanities that characterized the life of secular *milites*. The Templars, as real monks, cut their hair short and dressed in a very simple way. The Order was commanded by a Grand Master, who was supported by several superior officers: the Seneschal, the Marshal and the Turcopolier. The

Seneschal administered the properties of the Order in time of peace and acted as quartermaster in time of war; the Marshal was the overall commander of the Order's military forces; and the Turcopolier was at the head of the Turcopoles. The Order was structured on provinces, of which there were two at the beginning: one for the Holy City and one for the rest of the Kingdom of Jerusalem. Each province was commanded by a Master and was sub-divided into a series of smaller administrative entities known as preceptories. In terms of internal composition and organization, a Templar preceptory was comparable to a commandery of the Hospitallers. Each Templar knight was allowed to possess three horses and to have a squire with a fourth horse. The armour, clothing and bedding of each *miles* – however – belonged to the Order, and thus were not the private property of the knight. The squires were non-combatants, their main task on the battlefield being to take care of their lord's

Fatimid kite shield. (*Photo and copyright by Les Seigneurs d'Orient*)

Seljuk sword with straight blade. (*Photo and copyright by Les Seigneurs d'Orient*)

horses. Like the Hospitallers, soon after their establishment, the Templars received a flood of donations from Europe; as a result, by 1130, new preceptories could be created across the Mediterranean and further afield: Antioch, Tripoli, Aragon, Portugal, England, Aquitaine, Poitou, Provence, Apulia, Hungary, Germany, Sicily and Greece. The preceptories were used for recruiting and training new Templars, but also to administer the many properties owned by the Order. Indeed, at the peak of their power, the Templars had over 9,000 feudal lordships or manors throughout Europe (from which feudal knights and sergeants could be levied according to the sub-infeudation system). The military forces of the Templars gradually started to comprise sergeants in addition to knights; these were known as brother sergeants and had an inferior status compared with the *milites*, being subordinate to them. The Order also comprised the *confrère* knights, lay *milites* who became temporary members of the Templars for a specific period of time. The *confrère* knights were usually recruited for major military campaigns. They were permitted to marry, but had to promise that half of their personal property would go to the Order if they were killed in combat. By the middle of the twelfth century, the Templars were the major landowners of the Kingdom of Jerusalem and could provide 600 knights in time of war. Having great sums of money at their disposal, the Templars soon became successful bankers and started to lend money to most of the Crusader states' aristocrats. Pilgrims could deposit their funds in one preceptory of the Templars and withdraw them by producing letters of credit at any other Templar preceptory in the Mediterranean. Like the Hospitallers, the Templars were given several important strongholds in the Holy Land and had their own fleet, which was mostly employed to transport pilgrims but could also be used to conduct seaborne incursions against the Muslims. The Grand Master of the Templars and the Grand Commander of the Hospitallers were among the most important commanders of the Kingdom of Jerusalem's forces, their advice usually being followed by the various monarchs and their opinions rarely being questioned. The Templars and the Hospitallers were the finest Christian fighting forces in the Levant. When they went into battle with the army of the Kingdom of Jerusalem, the Templars were always accorded the position of honour on the right wing, while the Hospitallers were deployed on the left wing. The heraldry of the Templars consisted of a red cross placed on a white background.

Saracen scimitar. (*Photo and copyright by Les Seigneurs d'Orient*)

Teutonic Knights: During the Fourth Crusade, at the siege of Acre in 1190, a group of wealthy German merchants from the cities of Bremen and Lubeck set up a tented hospital to cure the many wounded and sick Crusaders from the Holy Roman Empire. The siege lasted for eight months, and by its end the temporary German hospital had become a permanent institution, which was supported financially by Emperor Henry VI. By 1196 the German hospitallers already had several branches in the Holy Land and had been recognized by the Pope as an independent monastic Order that was to follow the same rule as the Saint John's Order. In 1197, the new German Order decided to establish its own military branch, following the example of the Templars; as a result, it started to comprise warrior-monks who followed the same rules as the Templars. By 1199, the Pope had granted official recognition to the new Military Order, which became known as the Teutonic Order. As its name suggests, differently from the Templars and Hospitallers, who mostly consisted of French knights, it was a German organization. By 1220, the Teutonic Order already had twelve houses –

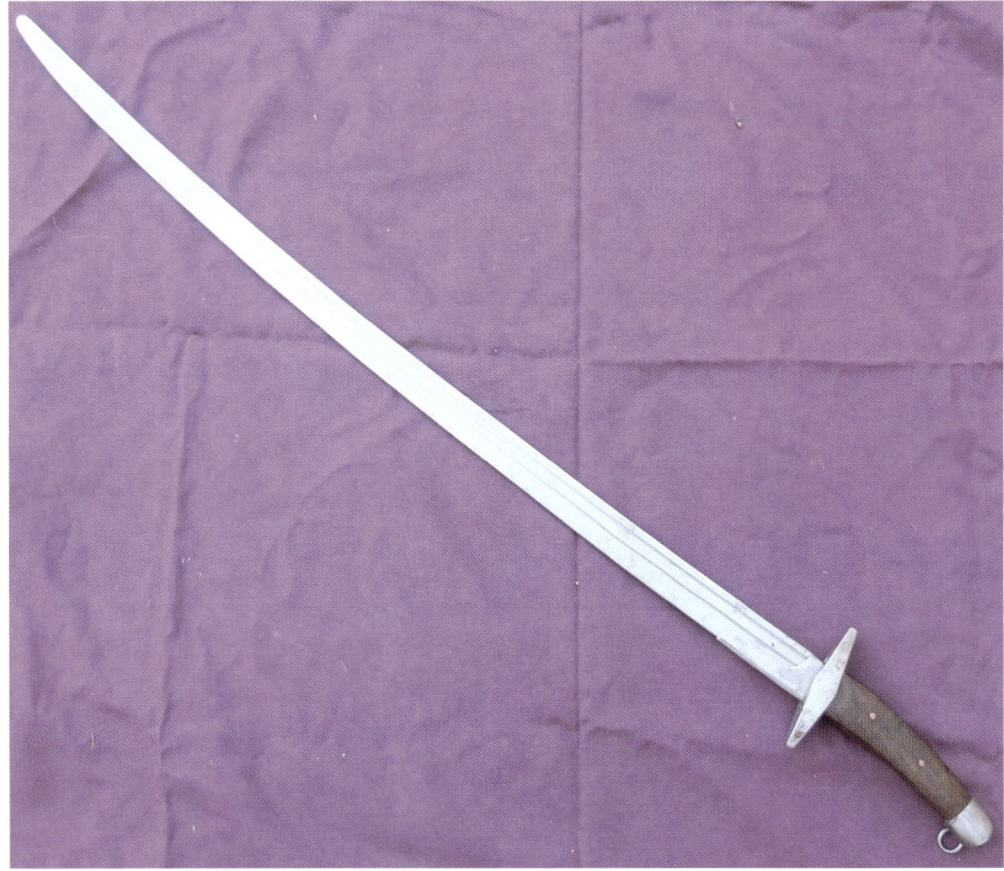

Saracen scimitar. (*Photo and copyright by Les Seigneurs d'Orient*)

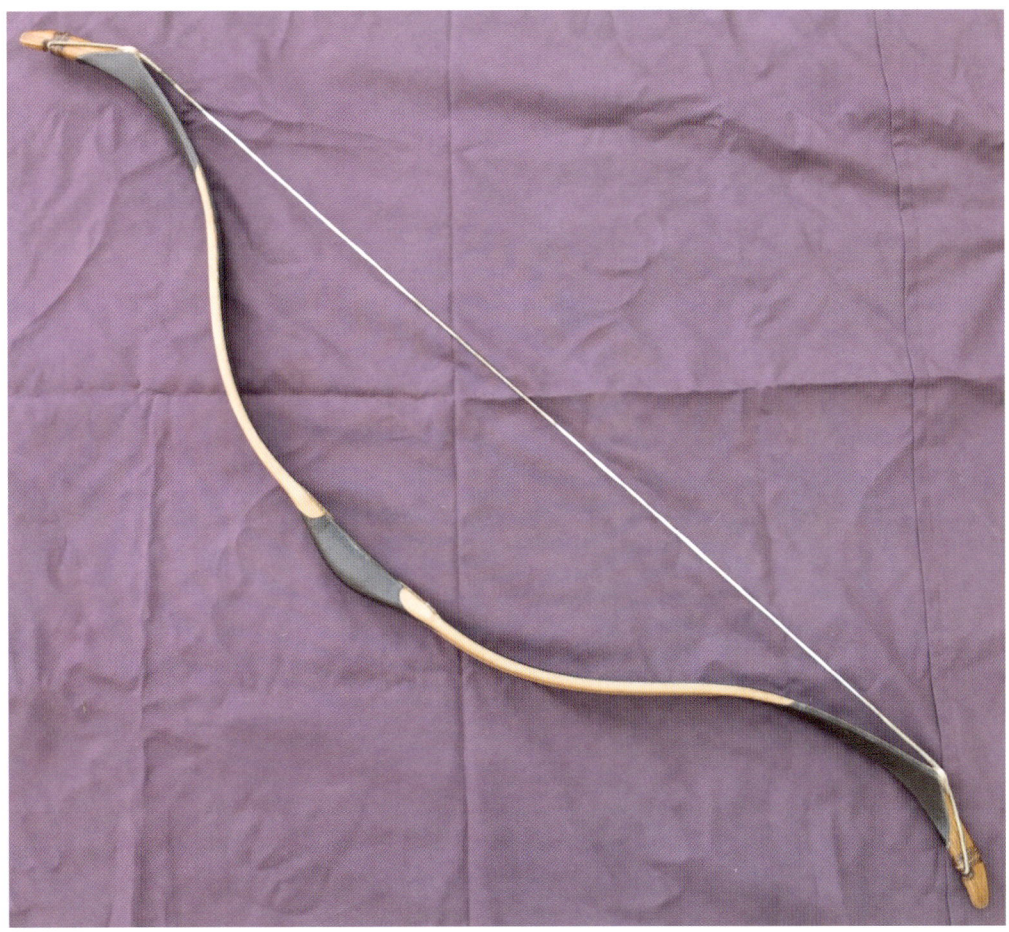
Seljuk composite bow. (*Photo and copyright by Les Seigneurs d'Orient*)

corresponding to the Templar preceptories – in Palestine, Greece, southern Italy and Germany. The various houses were grouped into provinces; each house, or *Komtureis*, consisted of twelve knights commanded by an officer known as a *Komtur*. At the head of the Order was the *Hochmeister* or High Master, who was supported by several superior officers: the *Gross Komtur*, who corresponded to the Templar Seneschal; the *Ordensmarschall*, or Marshal; the *Spittler*, who corresponded to the Hospitaller of the Order of Saint John; the *Tressler*, or Treasurer, who administered the economic resources of the Order; and the *Trapier*, who acted as quartermaster. Like the Templars and the Hospitallers, the Teutonic Knights also consisted of *milites* and brother sergeants. The Teutonic Order employed large numbers of mercenary knights and Turcopoles, just like the other two major Military Orders. Following the Templars' example, it also comprised temporary members known as Halbbruders. In 1226, Holy Roman Emperor Frederick II paid the Teutonic Order a great honour by making its *Hochmeister* and all his successors imperial princes, having the right to display the imperial eagle on their arms as official representatives of the Holy Roman Empire. When Frederick was crowned King of Jerusalem, it was the Teutonic Order that provided the guard of honour for the coronation ceremony in the Holy Sepulchre. Despite these successes, due to the presence of the Templars and the Hospitallers, the Teutonic Knights always had serious difficulty in obtaining prominence in the Holy Land. All the most important castles and lands of the region had already been granted to the other two Military Orders, so little space remained for their expansion. Compared with those of the Templars and the Hospitallers, the military forces deployed by the Teutonic Order in the Levant were always smaller (mustering around 300 knights and 450 sergeants). It should be noted, however, that from the beginning of the thirteenth century, the Teutonic Knights diverted most of their energies and resources away from the Holy Land as they started to conduct crusading expeditions in Eastern Europe and the Baltic. Both the Papacy and the Holy Roman Empire were greatly interested in Christianizing the pagan lands located on the north-eastern borders of Germany. It was in this 'wild north' that the Teutonic Knights fought their most famous battles and won their most glorious victories, becoming the dominant military power of the Baltic long after the Holy Land had been lost by the Crusaders. The heraldry of the Teutonic Order consisted of a black cross placed on a white background.

Bibliography

Bartlett, W.B., *Richard the Lionheart: The Crusader King of England* (Amberley Publishing, 2019).
Gravett, C., *English Medieval Knight, 1200–1300* (Osprey Publishing, 2002).
Gravett, C., *German Medieval Armies, 1000–1300* (Osprey Publishing, 1997).
Gravett, C., *Norman Knight, 950–1204* (Osprey Publishing, 1994).
Heath, I., *Armies and Enemies of the Crusades, 1096–1291* (Wargames Research Group, 1978).
Heath, I., *Armies of Feudal Europe, 1066–1300* (Wargames Research Group, 1989).
Nicholson, H., *Knight Templar, 1120–1312* (Osprey Publishing, 2004).
Nicolle, D., *Arms and Armour of the Crusading Era, 1050–1350* (Greenhill Books, 1988).
Nicolle, D., *French Medieval Armies, 1000–1300* (Osprey Publishing, 1991).
Nicolle, D., *Italian Medieval Armies, 1000–1300* (Osprey Publishing, 2002).
Nicolle, D., *Italian Militiaman, 1260–1392* (Osprey Publishing, 1999).
Nicolle, D., *Knight Hospitaller (1), 1100–1306* (Osprey Publishing, 2001).
Nicolle, D., *Knight Hospitaller (2), 1306–1565* (Osprey Publishing, 2001).
Nicolle, D., *Knight of Outremer, AD 1187–1344* (Osprey Publishing, 1996).
Nicolle, D., *Teutonic Knight, 1190–1561* (Osprey Publishing, 2007).
Nicolle, D., *The Crusades* (Osprey Publishing, 1988).
Nicolle, D., *The Normans* (Osprey Publishing, 1987).
Remo Vallejo, Y., *The Crusades* (AeroArt International, 2002).
Wise, T., *Armies of the Crusades* (Osprey Publishing, 1978).
Wise, T., *The Knights of Christ* (Osprey Publishing, 1984).

The Re-enactors who Contributed to this Book

Les Seigneurs d'Orient
The Lords of the Orient (Les Seigneurs d'Orient) is an historical re-enacting club based in Menton, France, since 2017. Our thirty-member club has a large proportion of history students and teachers. Our area of expertise is the twelfth-century Near East, and especially the Oriental Latin States (Outre Mer/Holy Land). We re-enact both Jerusalem's royal court and a Syrian Emir's court, with camp, furniture, civil and military outfits and workshops. We can cover projects from the First Crusade to the thirteenth century. The Lords of the Orient is part of the Living History Lovers Federation along with The Somatophylakes, re-enacting Greek and Macedonian phalanxes. We can thus gather more than forty fully equipped adults in a large camp. We take part in historical festivals and patrimonial exhibitions, and run conferences on feudal society and twelfth-century Oriental Latin states. We have been hired for television documentaries by Patrick Spica Productions–RMC Découverte (The secret of Monaco's Grimaldi fortress) and ZED production–Curiosity (The siege of Acre), and for book or magazine illustrations by such publishers as Pen & Sword Books and Heimdal édition. Our main activities include historical research, artefact fabrication, civil and military outfit building, sword-shield and lance-shield medieval fighting, military group movements and formations, camp life and public shows.

Contacts:
E-mail: cyril.errera@hotmail.com
Website: https://lesseigneursdorient.wixsite.com/lesite
Facebook: https://www.facebook.com/Lesseigneursdorient/

Ordenskomturei Heppenheim
We are a living history association focused on re-enacting the former Deutschordenskommende Weinheim. Currently, the re-enactment of the Kommende Weinheim consists of four knight brothers, three nuns and a sergeant, depicting costumes from a period between the thirteenth century and the early sixteenth century. We reconstruct both civil and military costumes, with full armour and weapons. Our group equipment includes one mobile altar, an armouring tent

and a field hospital. Networked all over the world, we have already pitched our camp at many events, both at friendship camps and many booked performances. The group's current Komtur (commander), as portrayed by member Oliver Bethke-Pohl, is Ullrych von Bykenbach, who was born in 1222 at Weiler Hügel Alsbach and died in 1268.

We would like to thank all our friends and supporters from the bottom of our hearts, and some we would like to mention here: Thomas Weinhold for the great pictures of his weapons, Burgschänke Schloss Alsbach Mirco and Kathrin, https://www.burgschaenkeaufschlossalsbach.de/, https://www.facebook.com/GaststaetteSchlossAlsbach; Burgverein Schloss Alsbach Christopher Teske, http://schloss-alsbach.org/, https://www.facebook.com/groups/296702357203777/; Helgard Meer and the Hanse Festival of the city of Neuss, https://www.facebook.com/helgard.meer; and Friends of Alsbach Castle. Donations for the preservation of the castle walls of Alsbach Castle are urgently needed. Every donation counts: Volksbank Weschnitztal e.G., IBAN: DE57509615920000199770, BIC: GENODE51FHO. Would you like to book us for your event? Organization, armour fencing and event planning are made by Oliver Bethke-Pohl.

Contacts:
E-mail: obethke@mail.de
Facebook: https://www.facebook.com/KommendeWeinheimOT
https://www.facebook.com/ordenskomturei.heppenheim.5

Sericum et ferrum
We are a re-enactment group focussing on Anglo-Norman lesser nobility in the time between 1180 and 1200. We try to reconstruct everything from clothes to armour as well as we can and always try to get better at what we are doing. Analysing historical sources and reading are the most important parts of our hobby, so we also support other authors wherever we can. Our goal is to teach history in a different and exciting way to everyone who is interested. We are located near Bremen in Germany and cooperate worldwide.

Contacts:
Facebook: https://www.facebook.com/Sericumetferrum

Index

al-Adil, 95, 99, 102, 104
Alphonse of Toulouse, 71
Amadeus III of Savoy, 71

Baibars, 114, 116, 120
Berengaria of Navarre, 88, 91

Conrad III, 68, 70, 71, 72, 73, 76
Conrad of Montferrat, 93
Constance of Hauteville, 88, 95

Daimbert of Pisa, 51

Gregory VII, 4, 7, 14, 84

Henry IV, 7, 14, 22
Henry of Marcy, 84
Honorius III, 101

Melisende, 64, 65, 77

Nur ad-Din, 68, 73, 76, 77, 80

Otto of Freising, 71, 73

Peter Bartholomew, 33, 37
Peter Desiderius, 43
Peter the Hermit, 17, 18, 19

Queen Joan, 88

Renaut I of Bar, 71
Robert Curthouse, 22, 36
Robert Guiscard, 22,
Roger II, 70, 72

Thierry of Alsace, 71

Urban II, 14, 15, 16, 47, 68

Welf I of Bavaria, 58
William IX of Aquitaine, 58
William V of Montferrat, 71
William VII of Auvergne, 71

Zengi, 64, 65, 68